Narratives of
Sullivan's Expedition, 1779

Narratives of
Sullivan's Expedition, 1779
Against the Four Nations of the Iroquois &
Loyalists by the Continental Army

John L. Hardenbergh
William McKendry
William Elliott Griffis
Simon L. Adler

LEONAUR

Narratives of Sullivan's Expedition, 1779
Against the Four Nations of the Iroquois &
Loyalists by the Continental Army
by John L. Hardenbergh
William McKendry
William Elliott Griffis
Simon L. Adler

First published under the titles
The Journal of Lieutenant John L. Hardenbergh
Journal of William McKendry: from 1779 Sullivan's Expedition
Against the Indians of New York
The New Hampshire Brigade in the Sullivan Campaign: from the
Annual Address 1910
and
Sullivan's Campaign in Western New York 1779

FIRST EDITION

Leonaur is an imprint of Oakpast Ltd

Copyright in this form © 2010 Oakpast Ltd

ISBN: 978-0-85706-395-3 (hardcover)
ISBN: 978-0-85706-396-0 (softcover)

http://www.leonaur.com

Publisher's Notes

The opinions of the authors represent a view of events in which he
was a participant related from his own perspective,
as such the text is relevant as an historical document.

The views expressed in this book are not necessarily
those of the publisher.

Contents

Biographical

John Leonard Hardenbergh, the author of the following *Journal*, was a native of Rosendale, Ulster County, in the Province of New York, born in the year 1748. He was the son of Leonard and Rachel Hardenbergh, and the youngest of seven children. The family name is one of the oldest in the State, and is prominent both in its colonial and revolutionary annals. As early as 1644, Arnoldus van Hardenbergh a "free merchant" emigrated from Holland to New Amsterdam "with a cargo of wares for sale in the colony." He was soon after selected as one of the original Nine Men of New Netherland, and served in this board from 1647 to 1650.[1] He was followed in, or about, the year 1652, by his brother Johannes van Hardenbergh, also a merchant from Amsterdam, who at this date was purchaser of "a house, lot and garden" on Manhattan Island. (Calendar, Hist. MSS. in office of the Secretary of State, Albany, Part 1, vol. 3).

The branch of the family that was subsequently settled at Rosendale, is traced to the year 1706, when Johannes Hardenbergh, with

---

1. The original Nine Men were selected by the Director-General from eighteen delegates chosen by the people, and composed of merchants, *burghers* and farmers. Six of the nine retired annually and their places were filled by appointment from twelve of the "most notable citizens." Their powers were advisory and limited, as they were only to give advice on such propositions as the Director or his council might submit to them. The object of establishing such a Board, and as rehearsed in the colonial charter, was

"That the colony, and principally New Amsterdam, our capital, might continue to increase in good order, justice, police, population, prosperity and mutual harmony; and be provided with strong fortifications, a church, a school, trading places, harbour, and similar highly necessary public edifices and improvements; that the honour of God and the welfare of our dear Fatherland to the best advantage of the Company and the prosperity of our good citizens be promoted; and that the pure reformed religion as it is here in the churches of the Netherlands may be inculcated and preserved."

six others, obtained from the crown of Great Britain a grant of land which comprised, as computed at the time, 1,500,000 acres, located in Northern Ulster, then including a portion of the present county of Sullivan,—the western boundary extending to, or near the head of, the Delaware River. The terminal syllable of the name, *bergh*, indicates that the earlier ancestors in Holland were from the hills; and it was quite natural that their descendants should have found permanent location in the hilly districts of Shendaken and Shawangunk, stretching westward from the valley of the Hudson; neither is it surprising that they should have loved freedom and have given their best efforts for its establishment in their adopted land.

At the outbreak of the Revolution, Colonel Johannes Hardenbergh, Jr. was placed at the head of the Committee of Safety for Ulster County—Kingston, its chief town, being at the time the seat of the New York Provincial Congress of which he was also a member. He had ranked as Colonel in the English colonial service, and been active in military affairs as early as 1748, when Sir William Johnson was in command of the New York troops for the defence of the frontier against the French and Indians. He was also given command by the Provincial Congress of one of the earliest regiments raised for the immediate defence of the Hudson above the Highlands, at the opening of the war of Independence, and from his experience and position was enabled to render distinguished service at that critical period. In 1786, three years after the return of peace, he removed from his farm in Rosendale to New Brunswick, N.J., to spend the remnant of his days with his son, Rev. Dr. Jacob R. Hardenbergh, the first President of Rutger's College.

Leonard Hardenbergh, a younger brother of Colonel Johannes, Jr., and the father of the subject of this sketch, died July 7, 1776, only three days after the adoption of the Declaration of Independence, and as his neighbours of the hardy yeomanry of Ulster, were leaving their harvests ungathered and marching to the defence of Fort Montgomery, one of the principal fortifications guarding the passes of the Hudson. In the official returns for the same month (July) the name of John L. Hardenbergh appears as First Lieutenant in the Second New York Militia under command of Colonel Morris Graham, and assigned to the Brigade of General George Clinton, who had remained in the Continental Congress to vote for the Declaration, when he hastened home to his command.

Having served several months in this regiment raised under special call, Hardenbergh was commissioned Nov. 21, 1776, First Lieutenant in the Second New York Continental Regiment, under Colonel Rudolphus Ritzema,[2] who was superseded Nov. 30, 1776, by the appointment of Colonel Philip Van Courtlandt, a gallant officer and a personal friend of Washington whose confidence he shared to an unusual degree.[3] The regiment had the previous month been in the battle of White Plains, under Lieutenant-Colonel Weissenfels, where it did some hard fighting; and was ordered by Washington to Fishkill for the winter, to be recruited and disciplined, and thus ready for active service in the Spring.

But few enlistments, however, were obtained, though several recruiting parties were sent out for the purpose; and in the Spring of 1777, it was ordered to Peekskill, a point for the collection of military stores, and where at this time large quantities had been gathered under protection of General McDougall's brigade. Soon after, a fleet of ten British ships or transports appeared in Peekskill Bay, and landed a force of five hundred men with four pieces of artillery, which compelled General McDougall, who had scarcely half that number of troops, to retreat to Gallows Hill, about ten miles in the rear, leaving what stores could not be removed, in the hands of the enemy, who remained in possession of the town until McDougall was reinforced, when they retired to their ships and returned to New York.

After several weeks of hard and perilous service, Colonel Van Courtlandt with his regiment, was ordered to Albany and thence to the relief of Fort Stanwix, then besieged by Colonel St. Leger with a party of Indians; but on information that the enemy had retired, he joined General Poor, then on the advance to Stillwater, to whose brigade the regiment became attached, and thus made a part of General Arnold's command, forming a portion of the left wing in the first bat-

---

2. Colonel Ritzema was a Hollander by birth, and educated as a soldier in the Prussian army. Being refused the advancement to which he deemed himself entitled, he left the American service, but not before he was suspected of disaffection, if not of treachery. During the battle of White Plains, where his regiment was engaged, he was some four or five miles away, and was shortly after displaced from his command. He subsequently joined the British army.
3. Colonel Van Courtlandt gives the following account of the manner of his appointment: "This commission was sent by General Washington, by express, and was of his own direction, having been furnished with blanks from Congress signed by John Hancock, President, for him to fill up as he thought proper, appointing me Colonel of the Second New York Regiment, dated November 30, 1776." *Autobiography, &c. The Magazine of American History for May, 1878.*

tle of Stillwater, which was fought on the 19th of September.

The loss of killed and wounded of the Second New York was two out of eleven, which was a larger proportion than of any other regiment engaged, the next largest being that of Colonel Cilley's First New Hampshire, which was one out of seven, all of General Poor's Brigade. At the second battle, which occurred on the 7th of October, the regiment sustained its reputation for determined bravery and hard fighting, and thus bore an honourable part in the most important engagement, thus far, of the war, the results of which changed the whole aspect of the American cause.

After the Battle of Stillwater, which compelled the surrender of Burgoyne, and rendered fruitless the previous successes of the enemy along the Hudson, the regiment returned to Fishkill, and soon joined the army under Washington, then confronted by the British forces under General Howe, in the vicinity of Philadelphia. It shared the privations and sufferings of the terrible winter encampment at Valley Forge, (1777-8) the march to which of the half naked, half-starved, shoeless army might be tracked in blood through the December snows. It appears from an orderly book[4] found among the papers of Colonel, afterwards General Henry Dearborn, also in the Sullivan expedition, that at Valley Forge, Hardenbergh was lieutenant and adjutant of his regiment and often served as adjutant of the day at headquarters.

The whole encampment consisted of about eleven thousand troops; and when it was broken up the following Spring, upwards of three thousand men unfit for duty were left behind, under charge of Colonel Van Courtlandt, while his regiment proceeded with the main army, and participated in the Battle of Monmouth, June 28, 1778, winning commendation for bravery and good behaviour in that hotly contested engagement.

While at camp with the main army at White Plains the same season, the Second New York Regiment was sent to guard the frontiers in Ulster County against the depredations of the Indians under Brant, who had already destroyed several houses and murdered men, women and children. It remained in the neighbourhood of Laghawack, on this duty, during the winter of 1778-79; and in the Spring while on the march to surprise Brant stationed on the Delaware with about one hundred and fifty Indians, an express from General Washington overtook the regiment with orders to proceed to Fort Penn, there to await orders from General Sullivan. It is at this point that the *Journal of*

4. Mss. in possession of Mr. John H. Osborne, of Auburn, N.Y.

Lieutenant Hardenbergh, herewith published, dates.

On its return from the Expedition, the regiment proceeded to Easton, Pennsylvania, and from thence to Morristown, N.J., where it was hutted for the winter. In the spring of 1780 it was sent to Fort Edward for temporary service, and in June proceeded to West Point, and in expectation of an attack from the enemy, was posted on the mountain west of Fort Putnam. This proved, however, to be a feint to cover an invasion of the Jerseys. During the treason of Arnold the regiment was at Tappan, whither Andre was taken after his capture, and where he was tried and executed.

From the autumn of 1776 to the winter of 1780, Lieutenant Hardenbergh was identified with the Second New York, sharing its fortunes, and participating in the important battles in which it was engaged, when the five New York regiments were consolidated into two, in which arrangement he fell into that class of officers who were retained in service but not attached to any battalion. But in July 1782 he was made Captain of Levies under Lieutenant Colonel Weissenfels, in which capacity he continued for the remainder of the war.

In the summer of 1781, he is accredited in the chronicles of the time, with a daring exploit, which indicates the kind of service in which he was engaged after he ceased to be attached to the Second New York. A body of three hundred Indians and ninety Tories under Captain Cauldwell, an officer in Butler's Rangers, appeared on the frontier of Ulster County, in the neighbourhood of Warwasing, having passed unobserved the stockade forts at the north of Lackawaxen and Neversink, expecting to surprise the settlements and repeat the scenes of massacre which had desolated other regions in the vicinity. Captain Hardenbergh, at the time, was stationed with a guard of nine[5] men, near the house of J.G. Hardenbergh,[6] and at a point some three miles distant from a small fortress at Warwasing.

---

5. Some accounts make the number even less.

6. This house was pillaged about the same time, and large quantities of clothing and vegetables taken by the Indians. One Indian, a chief, emerged from the scene of plunder, mounted on a horse taken from the stable, profusely arrayed in stolen apparel, with silver bands about his arms and a bunch of some forty silver broaches hanging about his person. He was discovered by some soldiers who were on the alert to get a shot at the invaders as they were leaving the place, when one levelled his rifle at him and fired. He was seen to lay over on his horse, but turning into the woods, disappeared. Sometime after, his body was found near the place where he was shot with his plunder still about him. *Narrative of Massacres and Depredations in Wawarsing, &c., &c., Rondout, 1846.*

11

As the enemy passed the fort just before the break of day they were fired upon by the sentinel. The report alarmed Captain Hardenbergh, who with his little band proceeded immediately in direction of the sound, and on his way met the enemy directing their course toward the settlement, which is now called Rochester. Nothing daunted he gave them battle; but being closely pressed he soon discovered that his retreat was cut off by a party of Indians who had gained his rear. In this dilemma the captain resorted to stratagem which admirably answered the purpose. It was as yet barely light, and turning aside in the woods with the little company, to conceal the smallness of his force, he took off his hat and huzzaed with all his might, at the same time advancing toward a small stone house nearby, and in face of the Indians, who supposing that the troops were coming up from Pinebush, took the alarm and skulked off in every direction.

But no sooner had Hardenbergh and his company reached the house, when the Indians discovering the ruse, poured a shower of bullets after them just as they were safely within the door. Here they found six militia men besides, making sixteen in all, and being well armed, made all preparations to hold their position against the invaders. With an axe they broke a series of loop-holes in the rear of the house and through the sides of the steep roof, thus commanding its approaches on all sides. The enemy advanced several times to carry the house by assault, but as some of their number were doomed to fall at every onset, they as often gave way, and at length were compelled to relinquish the attack, leaving thirteen dead upon the field. In the meanwhile the firing had aroused the neighbourhood, and Colonel Henry Pawling with a detachment of State Levies, stationed about six miles from the scene of action, hastened forward, but arrived too late to have a brush with the enemy, and only in season to capture a straggler, who had lingered for fruit, near an apple orchard.

Cauldwell was in full retreat, and though pursued by Colonel Pawling with his regiment of Levies and Colonel Cantine with a regiment of State Militia, for some days, finally escaped. The enemy, however, suffered severely and besides losing a number of men, were so near starvation that they were obliged to eat their dogs before they reached Niagara, the point from which they had started on their errand of pillage and murder. This was the last attempt of the kind made upon the frontier settlements, which had suffered so severely from repeated invasions of Indians and Tories during the Revolution. It was designed to be a finishing blow upon that region, and as we have seen, it was largely due to the bravery and military tact of Captain Hardenbergh that the stroke was averted.

At the close of the war, during the entire period of which he had been in active service, he returned to his native place, to share the fruits of Independence with peace, which he had done so much to secure. He had justly acquired the reputation of a brave and skilful officer, and his name still appears on the Roll of Honour in the cabinet of Revolutionary memorials kept at Washington's Headquarters at Newburgh. He was for a time on Washington's staff; and his whole record is that of a devoted patriot and a faithful soldier, at a time when the country needed every heart and hand for its defence.

In 1789, the Indian titles to most of the lands in the State of New York, having been extinguished, the Legislature provided for the survey of a certain portion of these lands, already set apart for the soldiers of the State, who had served in the war of the Revolution. This tract embracing 1,680,000 acres, and denominated the Military Tract, included the present counties of Onondaga, Cayuga, Seneca and Cortland, also the larger part of Tompkins with portions of Oswego and Wayne. It was surveyed into twenty-eight townships, containing each one hundred lots of six hundred acres.

Each private soldier and non-commissioned officer had one lot assigned him. The officers received larger shares in proportion to their rank. Colonel Hardenbergh was appointed on this survey, in immediate association with Moses Dewitt, brother of Simeon Dewitt, at the time Surveyor-General of the State, and was occupied in this work during the years 1789-90. His field books, neatly kept and carefully preserved, are now in possession of the Cayuga County Historical Society, one of several valuable donations from the family to the Society's archives. The lands which fell to him on the assignment of military bounties, were located in Onondaga, disposing of which, he purchased lot Forty-Seven, within the present limits of Auburn, from Ogden and Josiah Hoffman, and originally patented to Captain Thomas Doughty also of the Second New York.

The deed bears date Feb. 16, 1792, and the consideration was one hundred and eighty pounds N.Y. currency. Colonel Hardenbergh was familiar as a surveyor with its comparative advantages, for a settlement, and especially with its superior water power, and had already indicated the lot on his map of survey as a "good mill site." He came on to his lands the same year (1792) bringing with him several negro slaves, and built a bark shelter near the site of the present Hardenbergh

13

mansion, and on the spot where the City Hall now stands. He made a visit in the fall or winter of that year, to Rosendale and was united in marriage to Mary Bevier, also of one of the most substantial and prominent families of that part of the State, and soon after returned to make further preparations for a permanent home.

This year also he received a commission as Major in the Battalion of Herkimer County, having previously been appointed a Captain in a Battalion for Montgomery, which until 1791 included the counties of Herkimer and Tioga. He was also appointed, in 1793, by Governor George Clinton, his old Brigade commander on the Hudson in the beginning of the war, an Associate Justice for Herkimer County, and designated the same year as one of the three Commissioners to lay out and construct the Genesee Turnpike. His last military promotion was that of Lieutenant Colonel of a regiment of Militia in Onondaga County, in April, 1796, by Governor John Jay, and gave him the title of Colonel, by which he is most commonly known in the early annals of Auburn.

In 1794 he had completed a saw and grist mill, on the Owasco Outlet, near where the Stone Mill now stands, opposite the junction of Genesee and Market Streets, thus forming the nucleus of a settlement known as Hardenbergh's Corners until 1805, when it took the name of Auburn.

The death of his wife occurred in the Spring, a little more than a year after their marriage, leaving an infant daughter, and before his arrangements were complete for bringing them to their new home in the wilderness.

In 1795 a colony of ten families from Gettysburgh, Pa., made a settlement about three miles up the Owasco Lake, and at once organized a Reformed Protestant Dutch Church, which subsequently took corporate form and title, Sept. 23, 1796, at a meeting held at the house of Colonel Hardenbergh, who identified himself with this society in the faith and order of which he had been educated. His copy of the New Testament with the Psalms in a single volume, and in the Dutch language, is still preserved; and bearing on the fly-leaf, under his own signature, the same date with that of his first army commission, it shows the signs of ordinary use not only, but the unmistakable marks of the exposure and hardships incident to a soldier's life.

His second marriage, in 1796, was with Martina, daughter of Rœliff Brinkerhoff, one of the first deacons of the Owasco church, and the names of his two children by this marriage, Maria and John Herring, appear on the baptismal register of that church for the years 1798 and 1800. The only son, John H. Hardenbergh, was in subsequent years one of Auburn's most prominent and public spirited citizens. As the heir to the landed estate of his father, originally covering a large section of the territory now occupied by the city, his wise and generous policy toward purchasers of lots and tenants, contributed much to its growth and prosperity.

The lot, in the centre of the city, on which stands the First Presbyterian church, one of the most substantial and elegant structures of the kind in the State, if not in the country, was his gift, before he had become of age; as were also eight acres of land comprised in the spacious grounds occupied by the Auburn Theological Seminary. These and similar deeds of generous foresight, together with an amiable character and a blameless Christian life, preserve in esteem and honour the name so closely identified with the origin of our favoured city.

Colonel Hardenbergh died after a brief illness, on the 25th of April, 1806, in the 59th year of his age, and was buried with military honours in the North Street Cemetery. The Rev. David Higgins, then pastor of the Congregational Church of Aurelius, and the founder of the First Presbyterian Church of Auburn, preached the funeral sermon from the Epistle to the Philippians, 3; 20, 21: *For our conversation is in heaven; from whence also we look for the Saviour, the Lord Jesus Christ, who shall change our vile body that it may be fashioned like unto his glorious body according to the working whereby he is able even to subdue all things unto himself.* The horse bearing the sword and uniform of the deceased officer, was led by Harry Freeman, one of the colonel's slaves to whom he had given his freedom.

A long procession of military and citizens followed the remains to the grave. The whole scene was imposing, as a sincere tribute of the respect and esteem cherished for the man who had braved the perils of the then recent struggle for national independence, and with generous hand had laid the foundations, in the wilderness, of a well-ordered community. He had passed thirty years of his life as a soldier, a surveyor, and a pioneer settler, and had occupied the most responsible trusts in the rising settlement which owed to him its origin. He was moreover a great favourite with his fellow pioneers, and with all who were seeking new homes in the immediate vicinity, ambitious rather for the thrift of the place than for personal gains, or the promotion of selfish ends—forward and generous in all plans to establish religion, education, justice and good order, with whatever tended to the permanent prosperity and true character of the infant settlement.

He was not always careful of his own interests, and was sometimes imposed upon by those in whom he confided as if they were as trustworthy as himself. If a neighbour wanted a bushel or two of grain, he might be trusted to measure it himself and render his own account. In this way and in others characteristic of him, he doubtless now and then lost pecuniarily, but they gave him a strong hold upon the better and larger class of his co-pioneers, and a leading influence at this forming period in our history. Indeed, Auburn owes very much to the spirit, foresight and enterprise of its founder.

In person, Colonel Hardenbergh was tall, of swarthy complexion, robust frame, and is said to have been a most commanding figure on horseback, in his regimentals, on military occasions. He took an active part in the politics of the day, and was decided and open in the expression of his opinions. He was a warm friend and ardent supporter of Governor George Clinton, under whom he had served in the first year of the war, and whose confidence he largely shared in the distribution of military promotions and civil appointments. A sturdy patriot, a brave soldier, a civilian, honoured and trusted in public station and in private life, he has fairly won the gratitude with which communities are wont to remember their founders.

Introduction to Journals

The following is printed from the original manuscript, in possession of the family, in the handwriting of Lieutenant Hardenbergh, undoubtedly an original journal made by him during the campaign of General Sullivan against the Indians.

The route covered by the *Journal*, begins at Wawarsing, in Ulster County, New York, passing south-westerly along the Mine road and Delaware River to Stroudsburg, Penn.; thence westerly over the mountains, by the Sullivan road to Wilkesbarre; thence up the Susquehanna River to Tioga Point near present Athens, where General Clinton's brigade on August 22nd, joined the main army; thence up the Chemung River to present Elmira, and northerly to Havana; thence along the east shore of Seneca Lake to present Geneva, and by way of Canandaigua, Honeoye, and Conesus to the Genesee River near present Cuylerville, in Livingston County, where was found the great Seneca town of Chenandoanes, or Genesee Castle, the most westerly point reached by the expedition.

The return was over nearly the same route to Easton, and thence up the Delaware to Morristown, N.J., where the regiment went into winter quarters.

In addition to Lieutenant Hardenbergh's journal, will be found that part of the journal of Major Erkuries Beatty, which relates to the march of General Clinton's brigade from the valley of the Mohawk, down the Susquehanna River to join General Sullivan at Tioga Point.

On the return march, Sept. 20th, when the army reached Kanadasega, an Indian town near present Geneva, Lieutenant Colonel William Butler commanding the Fourth Pennsylvania regiment, was detached with six hundred men, with orders to proceed around the north end of Cayuga Lake, and devastate the Indian settlements on the east side. Thomas Grant accompanied this detachment; that portion of his journal which relates to the operations of this force, is also presented.

On the next day, September 21st, Lieutenant-Colonel Henry Dearborn commanding the third New Hampshire regiment, with two hundred and fifty men, was detached to proceed along the west shore of Cayuga Lake to complete the destruction in that quarter. That part of Colonel Dearborn's journal describing his operations on this march, also appears. The journals of Lieutenant Hardenbergh, Major Beatty and Colonel Dearborn, have not hitherto appeared in print.

Notes have been added mostly from contemporary writers illustrating the text, and giving descriptions of events and places mentioned, also introducing, at the proper place, descriptions of important matters referred to and described in other journals, but not appearing in any of the preceding.

Especial attention has been given to the descriptions of Indian towns, and it is confidently believed, that here for the first time, can be found, at least, an approximation to a complete list, and the exact location of the entire number destroyed. The descriptions in nearly all cases are from personal knowledge obtained by actual survey; the evidences of aboriginal occupation being plainly apparent.

The maps and descriptions of the battle field of Newtown, and of the Groveland ambuscade, it is believed will be an important addition to the literature of the campaign, and a valuable aid to those engaged in its study; and will present a more correct description of these important matters than has hitherto appeared in print. The conclusions reached, are the result of a most patient examination of all authorities accessible, and will be likely to stand the test of the most intelligent and critical scrutiny.

The list of journals and narratives relating to this campaign, though not as perfect as might be desired, will be found useful to those who wish to obtain authentic sources of information, and undoubtedly, many will be surprised to learn that so much original material is in existence and accessible.

The text of the several journals, has been followed literally, from the original manuscript when possible. Proper names, especially those of Indian towns, even in the same manuscript, are often found with material variations in spelling, and in many instances, different authors give entirely different names for the same place; in other cases wrong

18

names are applied, and frequently are transposed. The great Seneca town, on the Genesee River, is honoured with several distinct names, one of which has seventy variations in spelling; and Appletown has three distinct locations, several miles distant from each other. Care has been taken, to avoid confusion as much as possible, by explanations in the notes, and in the use of names most in accord with those in modern use.

Journal of the Campaign of the Year 1779, Commencing May 1st

Saturday, May ye first.—Drew out of our Winter Quarters at Wawasink[1] and encamped in a field near Jacobus Brown's at that place.

Sunday, May 2nd.—Laid still in camp.

Monday 3rd.—Drew provisions and prepared for a march.

Tuesday, 4th.—Struck our tents. Loaded our baggage in order to proceed on our march for Weyoming, but being alarmed by an express that the savages were murdering the inhabitants at Fantine Kille, about five miles in our front, Colonel Cortlandt marched to their assistance, but before we arrived at the place they were gone. At 4 in the afternoon returned to Wawasink and remained in houses.[2]

---

1. Wawarsing—An Indian word, said to signify "a black bird's nest," the name of a town and village in south-west part of Ulster County, N.Y., containing a post village of same name, located on Rondout Creek on the line of the Delaware and Hudson Canal. The surface of the town is mostly mountainous uplands, intersected by deep valleys. The Shawangunk Mountains extend along the east border, and spurs of the Catskills occupy the central and west parts, the highest peaks being from 2,000 to 3,000 feet above tide. The eastern and north-western parts are rocky and precipitous, and unfit for cultivation. There was a stone fort in the village on the site of B.C. Hornbeck's house. On Aug. 12, 1781, a large party of Tories and Indians under one Caldwell, appeared in the town with a design of falling upon Napanock, but being informed that the place was defended by cannon they came to Wawarsing before the inhabitants were up in the morning. Two men and a young woman discovered the enemy before they reached the fort, and the young woman succeeded in closing the door just in time to prevent it from being burst open by the savages. Finding further attack to be dangerous they dispersed and burned and plundered the out settlements, and next day withdrew laden with spoils. Several lives were lost on both sides and much property destroyed.—*The Indians—or Narratives of Massacres and Depredations on the frontiers of Wawarsink and Vicinity.*

2. "Colonel Cantine commanding a regiment of militia arrived (cont. next page)

21

Note.—Fantine Kill, a settlement, on a stream of that name, about a mile from the present village of Ellenville, in the town of Wawarsing, Ulster County. The attack was made at daybreak by a party of thirty or forty Indians under Brant, who came by the way of the Indian trail to Grahamsville, and from thence through the woods to the settlement. Widow Isaac Bevier and two sons were killed, also the entire family of Michael Socks, consisting of the father, mother, two sons who were young men, two children, and one or two others. They attacked the house of Jesse Bevier, but the inmates being good marksmen and having plenty of ammunition succeeded in defending themselves until Colonel Van Cortlandt came to their relief.

"As I was about marching from my encampment, having called in my guard, I discovered smokes rising from the village about six miles south, and a lad sent from its vicinity informed me that the Indians were there burning and destroying. It was occasioned by two of my men deserting in the mountains, when I received the order to return; for they went to Brant and informed him that I was ordered away, and he expected that I was gone. . . . . . On my approach Brant ran off. He had about one hundred and fifty Indians, and as I approached him, he being on a hill, and seeing me leaning against a pine tree waiting for the closing up of my men, ordered a rifle Indian to kill me, but he overshot me, the ball passing three inches over my head."— *Colonel Van Cortlandt's manuscript statement, 1825.*

"General, while you were standing by a large tree during that battle, how near to your head did a bullet come, which struck a little above you?"

The General paused for a moment, and replied—"About two inches above my hat."

Brant then related the circumstances. "I had remarked your activity in the battle," said he, "and calling one of my best marksmen, pointed you out and directed him to bring you down. He fired and I saw you dodge your head at the instant I supposed the ball would strike. But as you did not fall, I told my warrior that he had just missed you, and lodged the ball in the tree." Conversation between Brant and General Van Cortlandt—

during the day. I then pursued but could not overtake him, as he ran through a large swamp beyond the hill; and Colonel Cantine being also in pursuit, I returned, not having any prospect of overtaking him."—Colonel Van Cortlandt's statement, 1825.

Stone's life of Brant, II., 460, incorrectly located at the battle of Newtown.

Wednesday, 5th.—Remained in the Quarters of yesterday.

Thursday, 6th.[3]—At 7 in the morning loaded baggage, marched to Lurenkill[4] and halted at Broadhead's[5] for refreshment about two hours, and marched for Mamacotting,[6] where we arrived at 7 o'clock at night.

Friday, 7th.—At 4 struck tents, marched at 5, halted at Bashesland[7] for refreshment for about two hours, proceeded on our march. Crossed Denanasink[8] Creek at Dewitt's[9] and arrived at Major Decker's, crossed the creek with wagons and encamped in the field near Decker's house.

Saturday, May 8th.—Drew provisions; marched at about 11 o'clock and encamped at Haurnanack.[10]

Sunday, 9th.—Discharged four wagons which we had taken from Wawasink; loaded our provisions on board the canoes, sent them down

3. "The second day after, pursued my march to Fort Penn as ordered by the commander-in-chief, and there received General Sullivan's orders to make a road through the wilderness."—Colonel Van Cortlandt's statement, 1825.
4. The present name of a stream flowing south-easterly two miles south of Ellenville.
5. On the Lurenkill two miles south of Ellenville.
6. Present Wurtzboro in town of Mamacating on Sauthier's Map of 1779, said to have been named in honour of an Indian chief, is about fourteen miles south-west of Wawarsing. A block house was here occupied during the revolution.
7. West Brookville, formerly called Bashusville, near the southern line of town of Mamakating in Sullivan County. So called from a squaw named Bashe, who lived on the bank of the creek. The first house built was of stone and used as a fort.
8. Mahackamack or Neversink River, the crossing appears to have been near Cuddebackville in the town of Deer Park.
9. DeWitt—A brother of Mrs. James Clinton, the mother of DeWitt Clinton; where he is said to have been born, March 2, 1769, while Mrs. Clinton was on a visit with her brother. General James Clinton in 1763 raised and commanded a corps of two hundred men, called the Guards of the Frontier. This position called Fort De Witt was one of the posts occupied. Other accounts say he was born at the homestead of the Clinton family at Little Britain.
10. Now Port Jervis, formerly called Mohockamack Fork, at the junction of the Neversink and Delaware Rivers. The route taken appears to have been over the "*old mine road*" as it was called, constructed by the early Dutch settlers of Esopus to reach a copper mine in Walpack Township, Warren Co., N.J. It follows the Mamakating Valley, the first north of the Shawangunk mountains, and continues in that of the Mahackamack branch of the Delaware River, and penetrates the Minnisinks east of that river. The mine was about three miles north-west from Nicholas Depew's house.

the Delaware. At 8 o'clock in the morning began our march; marched to Esquire Vancamp's;[11] the weather very hot, we rested ourselves and marched for Decker's Ferry[12] on Delaware, where we arrived at sundown and encamped.

Monday, 10th.—Laid still for refreshment and washing.

Tuesday, 11th.—Struck tents and marched at 7 in the morning; got over the ferry, proceeded on our march; rested for refreshments, at Smithfield at or near Depew's,[13] at 5 p.m.; marched for Fort Penn where we arrived at dusk of the evening.

May 12th and 13th.—Laid still at Fort Penn[14] on account of rainy weather.

Friday, May 14th, 1779.—The weather clear, we received orders to march at 1 o'clock in the afternoon. Struck tents, marched for Learn's;[15] marched about five miles and encamped in the wood.

Saturday, 15th.—About 7 in the morning struck tents and marched to Learn's; pitched camp, and proceeded with a party to mend the road to Weyoming.[16]

---

11. John Adams, while attending Congress during its session at Philadelphia, as late as 1800, passed over this same "Mine Road" as the most eligible route from Boston to that city. He was accustomed to lodge at Squire Van Campen's in the Jersey Minnisinks.

12. Decker's Ferry at Flatbrookville, about thirteen miles from Fort Penn at Stroudsburg.

13. Samuel Depew's, in the town of Smithfield, Monroe Co., Pa., on the west side of the Delaware, three miles above the Water Gap, where he settled prior to 1730. He was one of the Walloons who came to New York about 1697. Rev. H.M. Muhlenberg, who lodged at his house in 1750, states he had been Justice of the Peace, was a prominent man in Smithfield, and at that time advanced in life. The river is fordable at the head of Depew's Island, a little above the house. The old homestead is still in the Depew family; Nicholas, one of Samuel's sons, is well known in provincial history between 1750 and 1770. On the Pennsylvania side of the river on Depew's land, stood the *Smithfield* or old *Shawne* church, removed about 1854.

14. Fort Penn, at Stroudsburg, Monroe County, Pa., built in 1763, on the site previously occupied by Fort Hamilton, built in 1755

15. Larned's log tavern, north-west of Stroudsburg, twenty-eight miles from Easton. The main army encamped here June 19th, at camp called Pocono Point. This was the last house on the road between Easton and Wyoming. On the 3rd of July, 1781, Mr. Larned was shot and scalped near his house, as also was his son George. Another son, John, shot one of the Indians who was left on the spot where he fell. The Indians carried off George Larned's wife, and an infant four months old, but not wishing to be encumbered with the child, dashed out its brains.

16. The 2nd New York Regiment, Colonel Van Cortlandt, and Colonel Spencer's N.J. Regiment were ordered to precede the army and (continued next page)

Sunday, 16th.—Our camp remained, and were joined by Colonel Spencer's[17] regiment; we continued making the road. At night seven men deserted from our regiment.[18]

Monday, 17th.—Decamped from Learn's about 7 in the morning, and encamped at about 7 o'clock in the afternoon, just on the west side of a small creek called White Oak Run.[19]

Tuesday, 18th.—Our camp remained; we continued working on the road; I was ordered to remain in camp with the guard.

Wednesday, 19th.—Last night about 11 o'clock, an alarm happened by the firing of one of the sentinels, but soon found it to be false alarm, (see note following). The weather being wet, we remained in camp all day.

construct a road over the mountains to Wyoming. They followed the well known Indian trails mainly, one of which led from Easton by way of the Wind Gap, directly north, along the high lands between the Delaware and Susquehanna rivers, to New York State line near Oghquaga; the other leaving Fort Penn at Stroudsburg, passed through the townships of Pocono, Tunkhanna, Tobyhanna, Buck, Bear Creek, to Wyoming. Much of this road is still in use and is known as the "old Sullivan road." At Easton General Sullivan published the following order: Headquarters, Easton, May 31, 1779. ...The commander-in-chief returns his most sincere thanks to Colonels Cortlandt and Spencer, and to the officers and soldiers under their command for their unparalleled exertions in clearing and repairing the road to Wyoming. He cannot help promising himself success in an expedition, in which he is to be honoured with the command of troops who give such pleasing evidence of their zeal for the service, and manifest so strong a desire to advance with expedition against the inhuman murderers of their friends and countrymen. . . Order Book Lieu.-Colonel George C. Barber, of 3rd N.J. Regt., Adjutant General of the Western Army.
17. Colonel Oliver Spencer, Commanding the Independent regiment, 5th Continental of New Jersey.
18. General Sullivan reached Wyoming with the main body of the army June 23rd; the following appeared in orders on the 25th: Headquarters, Wyoming, June 25, 1779. .....At a general court martial held on the eighth instant, whereof Major Fish was president, Oliver Arnold of the 2nd New York regiment, was tried for desertion, found guilty, and sentenced to be shot to death; the General approves the sentence and orders it to be executed at the head of the regiment tomorrow afternoon at six o'clock. Edward Tyler of the same regiment tried by the same court for desertion, found guilty and sentenced to run the guantelope through Cortlandt's, Spencer's and Cilley's regiments, with a centinel at his breast to regulate his pace; the General approves the sentence and orders it executed tomorrow afternoon at five o'clock. John Stevens of the same regiment, tried for desertion, found guilty and sentenced to receive one hundred lashes; the General approves the sentence and orders it executed at the head of the regiment, tomorrow afternoon at six o'clock. ...Order Book, Lieu.-Colonel George C. Barber, Adjutant General of the Western Army.
19. Near the west line of Pocono Township, also called Rum Bridge.

Note.—There were three paths leading eastward from Wyoming; the southern, called the "warriors' path," by way of Fort Allen and along the Lehigh to the Delaware Water Gap at Easton; the northern, by way of the Lackawana at Capouse Meadows, through Cobb's Gap and the Lackawaxen, to the Delaware and Hudson; the middle one, along which this military road was constructed, led through the Wind Gap to Easton. The massacre of Wyoming in 1778 had filled the forests along this central trail with hundreds of helpless fugitives; some estimate the number about two thousand, mostly women and children; many sunk under the tomahawk, others died of excitement, fatigue, hunger and exposure; many were lost and perished in the woods, while hundreds were never seen or heard of after their precipitate flight.

At this time small parties of Indians still hovered around Wyoming. They watched the passes, and occasionally exhibited extraordinary instances of courage and audacity. Major Powell, with two hundred men of a regiment that had suffered severely at the battle of Germantown, having been ordered to Wyoming, arrived at Bear Creek about ten miles from that point, on the 19th of April. Deeming themselves out of danger from a surprise by the Indians, officers and men arrayed themselves in their best apparel, burnished their arms and put everything in shape for a respectable appearance on entering the Valley. According to the fashion of the day the officers donned their ruffles, powdered their hair, and with enlivening strains of music, advanced toward their destination.

The advance guard reported having seen some deer, and Captain Davis, Lieutenant Jones and others, started in pursuit; near the summit of the second mountain by the Laurel Run, and about four miles from the fort, a fire was opened upon them by the Indians in ambush. Davis, Jones, Corporal Butler and three soldiers were killed and scalped. Chaplain Rogers says:

> Scalped, tomahawked and speared by the savages, fifteen or twenty in number; two boards are fixed at the spot where Davis and Jones fell, with their names on each. Jones's being besmeared with his own blood. In passing this melancholy vale, an unusual gloom appeared on the countenances of both officers and men without distinction, and from the eyes of many, as by a sudden impulse,

26

drops the sympathizing tear. Colonel Proctor, out of respect to the deceased, ordered the music to play the tune
of *Roslin Castle*, the soft and moving notes of which,
together with what so forcibly struck the eye, tended
greatly to fill our breasts with pity, and to renew our
grief for our worthy departed friends and brethren.

The bodies of the two officers were exhumed a few weeks after
this and re-interred at Wilkesbarre, with military and Masonic
honours by the officers of Sullivan's army.

Thursday, 20th.—Rainy weather with some thunder; we remained
in camp.

Friday, 21st.—Foggy, rainy weather with thunder and lightning;
remained in camp. This day Ensign Swartwout[20] arrived in camp from
the State of New York, brought news that the Indians were lurking
about Rochester and Wawasink; and the inhabitants chiefly moved off
their families.

Saturday, 22nd.—The weather continued rainy. Remained in camp.
At sunset the weather cleared off.

Sunday, 23rd.—The morning fair and clear. Received orders to
march. At 8 o'clock the General beat; struck tents, proceeded on our
march till over a creek in the Great Swamp[21] called Tackhanack, the

---

20. Barnardus Swartwout, an ensign in first company of Colonel Van Cortlandt's
regiment.

21. "*Monday, June 21, 1779.*—This day we marched through the Great Swamp, and
Bear Swamp. The Great Swamp, which is eleven or twelve miles through, contains
what is called on our maps "shades of death," by reason of its darkness; both swamps
contain trees of amazing height, *viz.*, hemlock, birch, pine, sugar maple, ash, locust,
etc. The roads in some places are tolerable, but in other places exceeding bad, by
reason of which, and a long though necessary march, three of our wagons and the
carriages of two field pieces were broken down. This day we proceeded twenty
miles and encamped late in the evening at a spot which the commander named
Camp Fatigue. The troops were tired and hungry. The road through the swamps is
entirely new, being fitted for the passage of our wagons by Colonels Cortlandt and
Spencer at the instance of the commander-in-chief; the way to Wyoming, being
before only a blind, narrow path. The new road does its projectors great credit,
and must in a future day be of essential service to the inhabitants of Wyoming and
Easton. In the Great Swamp is Locust Hill, where we discovered evident marks of a
destroyed Indian village. Tobyhanna and Middle Creeks empty into the Tunkhanunk;
the Tunkhanunk empties into the head branch of the Lehigh, which at Easton, empties into the Delaware. The Moosick mountain, through a gap of which we passed
in the Great Swamp, is the dividing ridge which separates the Delaware from the
Susquehanna."—[*Rev. William Rogers' Journal.*]

road very bad, the baggage could not come up; went back and mended the road and encamped where the baggage was. In the evening, Sergeant Jonas Brown[22] with five men, was sent off to Weyoming with letters from General Sullivan to General Hand.[23]

Monday, 24th.—About 9 o'clock in the morning struck camp, marched across the Tackhanack[24] and encamped on a hight, about half a mile from the creek, but continued making the road which was very bad about that place.

Tuesday, 25th.—Left our camp standing, and continued making the road; built a bridge and causeway at Tobehanna[25] of one hundred and fifteen paces in length. The creek is considerable large and abounds with trout.[26] Some good land along the creek; the road very difficult to make.

Wednesday, 26th.—Laid still in camp on purpose to refresh the men, and washing. Sergeant Brown returned from Weyoming.

Thursday, 27th.—Went out to work.

Friday, 28th.—Finished the bridge across the Tobehanna and returned to camp.

Saturday, 29th.—John Curry and Michael Sellers were tried at the

---

22. Sergeant Jonas Brown, of Captain Charles Graham's Co., Second New York, returned as dead by Lieutenant Conolly, in 1785, drew lot twenty-three, of the military tract in Homer, containing six hundred acres.

23. Brigadier General Edward Hand, the youngest brigadier of the expedition. Born in Ireland the last day of 1744, was an ensign in the British army, served two years with his regiment in America, then resigned and settled in Pennsylvania. At the beginning of the Revolution he entered the continental service as lieutenant-colonel, was made colonel of a rifle corps in 1776, was in the battles of Long Island and Trenton, and in the summer of 1777 was in command at Pittsburg. Washington placed great confidence in his judgment and consulted him freely as to the feasibility of this campaign. In 1780 he succeeded Scammel as Adjutant General of the army and held the position until the close of the war. He was a lover of fine horses and an excellent horseman. He died in Lancaster, Pa., Sept. 3, 1802.

24. Tunkhanna, from *Tankhanne, i.e., the small stream*, is a tributary of the Tobyhanna, which it enters at the west corner of Tunkhanna township. The smallest of two confluents or sources of a river is always called *Tankhanne* by the Delawares.

25. Tobyhanna, corrupted from *Topi-hanne*, signifying *alder stream, i.e.*, a stream whose banks are fringed with alders; is a tributary of the Lehigh, which it enters from the south-east at Stoddartsville.

26. The camp of the two regiments on White Oak Run, or Rum Bridge as called in some journals, was the same place where the main army encamped June, 19th, and "called Chowder Camp from the commander-in-chief dining this day on chowder made of trout."

drum-head, for stealing rum from the commissary[27] found guilty, and sentenced to receive, Curry seventy-five lashes, and Sellers fifty, which was directly put in execution. Our camp remained; we continued work on the road. After we returned from fatigue, General Sullivan and Colonel Hoopes[28] arrived in our camp.

Sunday, 30th.—In the morning General Sullivan and Colonel Hoopes returned to Easton. At 7 o'clock in the morning struck tents, the regiment marched to Locust Hill and encamped there;[29] myself was ordered to remain with the commissary stores which could not move with the baggage for want of teams.

Monday, 31st.—The colonel sent the wagons back to fetch the stores. We loaded them on the wagons and proceeded to camp and arrived there at 2 o'clock in the afternoon. The troops worked on the road.

Tuesday, June 1st.—Worked on the road. The camp remained on Locust Hill.

Wednesday, June 2nd.—Lt. Weissenfels[30] of our regiment was sent to Weyoming as an escort to guard a number of pack horses. The troops

27. "One quart of whiskey to be issued this evening to each officer, and a half pint to each non-commissioned officer and soldier on the detachment command by General Poor......The officers are to see respectively *that water be immediately mixed with the soldier's whiskey,*" General orders, Aug. 15, at Tioga.

28. Major Adam Hoops, third A.D.C. to General Sullivan. He was in the army throughout the Revolution, and at one period belonged to the staff of Washington. He was connected with the earliest surveys of Western New York. In 1804, he in company with Ebenezer F. Norton, purchased most of the township of Olean and laid out the village of Hamilton, the original name of present village of Olean. He was a bachelor and died in Westchester, Pa.

29. Dr. Jabez Campfield of Colonel Spencer's Regiment, joined his regiment while they were in camp at Tunkhanna on the 26th of May, where he says they continued until the 30th, "when we marched to Locust Hill. All this way the land very indifferent and rough, the timber mostly pitch pine and hemlock, some white pine, also birch, mirtle, and some beach, elm and spruce. This hill is covered with small locust trees. While the detachment remained at Locust Hill, the First New Hampshire Regiment joined us, but at the same time a detachment under Colonel Smith were sent to Wyoming so that we gained very little by the Hampshire men coming up." William Barton's *Journal* under date of June 11th says:
"Locust Hill so called, on account of being entirely timbered with it for twenty-three miles. We all proceeded on our journey again until we fell in with a detachment composed of several regiments which had been cutting a road through from Larnard's to Wyoming, as there never was any before only an old Indian path."

30. Lieutenant Charles F. Weissenfels of 3rd company, 2nd regiment, served during the war.

continued working the road. I was ordered on court martial, of which Captain Graham was President.

Thursday, June 3rd.—The troops did not work for want of provision.

Friday, June 4th.—The camp remained on Locust Hill. Captain Graham, myself, and two other officers were ordered to inspect pork which was chiefly condemned on account of its being spoiled.[31] On the 3rd of June, John Ten Eyck, soldier in Captain French's company of light infantry was drowned in the Lehi by accident.

Saturday, 5th.—The regiment was ordered on fatigue with three days provisions, that night lay out in the woods.

Sunday 6th.—I was relieved by Lt. Fairlie[32] and went to camp, this day we worked through the great swamp.

Monday, 7th June.—At about 8 in the morning decamped from Locust Hill, crossed the Lehi and encamped on the side of a Swamp called the Shades of Death,[33] about six miles from Locust Hill.

Tuesday, 8th June.—About 2 o'clock in the afternoon, struck our tents, marched through the Shades of Death, and encamped at night about one mile from the Shades.

Wednesday, 9th.—The camp remained.

Thursday 10th.—The camp remained. The troops worked on the road.

---

31. On the 21st of July, General Sullivan writes to Congress from Easton, after complaining of the delays of the quarter-master and commissary departments in forwarding supplies, he speaks as follows in regard to the quality: . . . . "My duty to the public, and regard to my own reputation, compel me to state the reasons why this army has been so long delayed here, without advancing into the enemy's country. . . . .The inspector is now on the ground, by order of the Board of War, inspecting the provisions; and his regard to the truth must oblige him on his return to report that, of the salted meat on hand, there is not a single pound fit to be eaten, even at this day, though every measure has been taken to preserve it that possibly could be devised. . . . . . About one hundred and fifty cattle sent to Sunbury were left there, being too poor to walk, and many of them unable to stand."

32. Lieutenant James Fairlie, of Captain Fowler's company, 2nd regiment, after the consolidation of the five New York regiments in 1780. He drew military lots Nos. seventy-three Cato, and sixty-five Brutus.

33. Shades of Death, supposed by many to have derived the name from the sufferings of those who escaped from the massacre of Wyoming, but this is evidently an error, as the name was attached to the locality and appeared on the maps, long previous to 1778.

Friday, 11th.—The regiment decamped and marched within seven miles from Weyoming. Captain Wright and I remained behind to guard the Commissary Stores.

Saturday, 12th.—The guard and Commissary Stores came up to camp.

Sunday, 13th.—Laid still.

Monday, 14th.—At six o'clock the General beat, struck tents and marched to Weyoming, (see note following), and arrived there at about 12, and pitched camp.

Note—Wyoming.

> *On Susquehanna's side, fair Wyoming!*
> *Delightful Wyoming!*—Campbell.

The Delaware name given to a valley on the Susquehanna River, of three to four miles in width, by about sixteen in length, extending from the mountain range above the Lackawana, where the river wends its way through a gorge a thousand feet deep, south-westerly to where the river again finds its way through a range equally lofty and precipitous. This was the Schahentoa or Schahen-dowane of the Iroquois, signifying *great plains*, as does also the Delaware name of Wyoming. From its earliest known history, this valley has been a favourite place of Indian residence, and was the probable seat of an Iroquois tribe, called Schahentoar-ronons by Brebeuf in 1635, whom he describes as allies of the Hurons, and speaking their language.

In 1614, three Dutchmen in the employ of the Directors of New Netherland, accompanied a party of Mahican Indians from near Fort Orange, in a war expedition against the Carantouannais, a powerful Iroquois tribe, whose main village containing more than eight hundred warriors, was located on the so-called "Spanish Hill" near Waverly, N.Y. These Dutchmen were captured by the Carantouannais, and were the first white men these Indians had ever seen; believing them to be French, who were allies of their friends the Hurons, they treated them kindly, and conducted them down the Susquehanna to this point, and thence by way of the Lehigh River, to the Delaware, where they were ransomed by Captain Hendricksen, "giving for them kittles, beads and merchandise."

In the map made by the captain from information furnished by these Dutchmen, he indicated four towns on the west side of the river, at this point, and designated the tribe as Minquas, this being the general name applied by the Dutch to all the Iroquois tribes south of the Five Nations, and west of New Netherland, several of which are known to have been in existence at that early date, but which appear to have been entirely overlooked by the scholars of the country.

June 15th and 16th.—Laid still.

Thursday, 17th.—Moved the camp about four miles up the River, to a placed called Jacob's Plains.[34]

18th and 19th.—Laid still.

Sunday, June 20th.—I was ordered to go down the River Sisquehannah with a party in boats[35] under the command of Captain Graham. Left Weyoming about 7 o'clock in the morning and arrived with the boats at Fort Jenkins[36] at sunset and stayed that night.

Monday, 21st.—Left Fort Jenkins in the morning, proceeded down the river and arrived at Northumberland town,[37] dined there, and proceeded to Sunbury and arrived there at 7 o'clock at night.

Tuesday, 22nd.—Laid still at Sunbury and loaded the boats with flour and beef.

Wednesday, 23rd.—At 9 o'clock in the morning left Sunbury, proceeded up the river about eight miles.

Thursday, 24th.—Proceeded up the river till night and lodged on board the boat. In the night lost my hat.

Friday, 25th.—Proceeded up the river as far as Fort Jenkins and

34. Jacob's Plains.—A *plateau* on the east side of the river, above present Wilkesbarre in the town of Plains. Abraham's Plains are on the west side of the river. "June 17.—Decamped at 10 o'clock. The three regiments marched up to Jacob's Plains, encamped near the bank of the river on the east shore, about four miles above the garrison."—*Nathaniel Webb's Journal.*

35. "*July 20.*—Three hundred boats arrived with provisions from Sunbury.
July 21.—Eight hundred head of cattle, five hundred horses, five hundred wagons arrived.
July 24.—Two hundred boats arrived, with stores, at which time thirty cannon were fired from the park."—*Nathaniel Webb's Journal.*

36. Fort Jenkins,—near Centreville, Columbia County, half way between Wyoming and Sunbury, built in 1777. There was another Fort Jenkins on the west side of the river a mile above Fort Wintermoot, built in 1776 under the supervision of the Jenkins and Harding families. This was captured and destroyed in 1778 in the Wyoming massacre.

37. Northumberland,—at the junction of the west, and main branches of the Susquehanna, above Sunbury, sixty-five miles from Wilkesbarre.

lodged there.[38]

Saturday, 26th.—Left Fort Jenkins and arrived at the falls.[39] Got half the boats up the falls, which were drawn up by ropes.

Sunday, 27th.—Got up the rest of the boats, and proceeded up the river and halted along shore over night. Colonel Ogden's regiment from Jersey was sent down as a guard to us from Weyoming.

Monday, 28th.—At Revelle beat proceeded up the river to the upper falls. Got all the boats up, (one of which overset in going up) and arrived at Shawny flats about four miles from Weyoming.

Tuesday, 29th.—Left Shawny flats in the morning and arrived at Weyoming[40] about 7 o'clock in the morning, unloaded the boats and went up to camp in the afternoon to Jacob's Plains.

Wednesday, 30th June.—The regiment was mustered in camp at Jacob's Plains. While I was out on my voyage down the river, General Sullivan arrived at Weyoming with troops to be employed on the ex-

---

38. During the absence of Lieutenant Hardenbergh down the river a party visited the battleground. "The place where the battle was fought may with propriety be called 'a place of skulls,' as the bodies of the slain were not buried, their bones were scattered in every direction all around; a great number of which for a few days past having been picked up, were decently interred by our people. We passed a grave where seventy-five skeletons were buried; also a spot where fourteen wretched creatures, who, having surrendered upon being promised mercy, were nevertheless made immediately to sit down in a ring, and after the savages had worked themselves up to the extreme of fury in their usual manner, by dancing, singing, halloaing, &c., they proceeded deliberately to tomahawk the poor fellows one after another. Fifteen surrendered and composed the ring; upon the Indians beginning their work of cruelty, one of them providentially escaped, who reported the matter to Colonel Butler, who upon his return to Wyoming, went to the spot and found the bones of the fourteen lying as human bodies in an exact circle."—*Rev. William Rogers' Journal.*
39. Nescopec Falls—at present Nescopec in county of Luzerne.
40. "Wyoming is situated on the east side of the east branch of the Susquehanna, the town consisting of about seventy houses, chiefly log buildings; besides these buildings there are sundry larger ones which were erected by the army for the purpose of receiving stores, &c., a large bake and smoke houses. There is likewise a small fort erected in the town, with a strong abbata around it, and a small redoubt to shelter the inhabitants in case of an alarm. This fort is garrisoned by 100 men, draughted from the western army, and put under the command of Colonel Zebulon Butler. I cannot omit taking notice of the poor inhabitants of the town; two thirds of them are widows and orphans, who, by the vile hands of the savages, have not only deprived them of tender husbands, some indulgent parents, and others of affectionate friends and acquaintances, besides robbed and plundered of all their furniture and clothing. In short, they are left totally dependent on the public, and are become absolute objects of charity."—*Hubley's Journal.*

pedition.[41]

Thursday, July 1.—Laid still.

Friday, July 2nd; Saturday, July 3rd.—Remained at Jacob's Plains.

Sunday, July ye 4th.—Decamped from Jacob's Plains, crossed the River Sisquehannah and encamped on the west side the river, near forty fort[42] on a fine plain called Abraham's Plains.

Monday, 5th July.—Went out on a scouting party in order to hunt. Went up the river as far as Laghawanny Creek and returned at sunset. Met with no success.

During our stay at Weyoming we had nothing to do but to keep guard, and disciplining our troops; only a few that were employed in boating to carry provisions[43] up the river from Sunbury to Weyoming.

(From July 5th to July 31st no entry was made in the *Journal*).

Saturday, the 31st of July.—About 3 o'clock in the afternoon we left Weyoming on our expedition. Our baggage being carried on pack horses, the provisions and artillery in boats, we marched as far as Lackawannick,[44] ten miles from Weyoming, and encamped.[45]

Sunday, Aug. first.—At 1 o'clock in the afternoon struck our tents

41. The army when concentrated at Wyoming was organized as follows New Jersey Brigade, Brigadier General William Maxwell commanded.-1st N.J., Colonel Matthias Ogden.-2nd, N.J., Colonel Israel Shreve, 3rd, N.J., Colonel Elias Dayton, 5th, N.J., Colonel Oliver Spencer's Independent Regiment, also fragments of Forsman's and Sheldon's regiments merged into Spencer's.—New Hampshire Brigade, Brigadier General Enoch Poor, commanded, 1st N.H., Colonel Joseph Cilley, 2nd N.H., Lieutenant Colonel George Reid, 3rd N.H., Lieutenant Colonel Henry Dearborn, 2nd N.Y., Colonel Philip Van Cortland.—Brigade of Light Troops, General Edward Hand, commanded, 11th Pa., Lieutenant Colonel Adam Hubley, German Regiment, Major Daniel Burkhardt, Independent Wyoming Company, Captain Simon Spalding, Wyoming Militia, Captain John Franklin, Schott's Rifle Corps, under Captain Selin.

42. Forty Fort—On the right bank of the Susquehanna between Pittston and Wilkes-barre, built in 1770 by the company of emigrants from Connecticut, forty in number.

43. General Hand, and other officers were engaged for six weeks in collecting supplies, which General Sullivan expected would be in Wyoming on his arrival. Four hundred and fifty boatmen were enlisted and large parties of soldiers were detailed for this service.

44. Lackawanna River, flowing into the Susquehanna from the north-east, called by the Delawares, *Lechau-Hanneck*, signifying the forks of a river or stream, and by the Iroquois *Hazirok*; an Indian town called Adjouquay existed at an early date on the east side, on present site of Pittston.

45. Falling Springs.—A short distance above Campbell's ledge, (cont. next page),

and marched seven miles to a place called Quialutimack.[46] The road was very difficult, the baggage did not arrive till towards day.

Monday, August ye 2nd.—Laid still at Quialutimack.

Tuesday, Aug. 3rd.—At 7 o'clock in the morning struck our camp, loaded our baggage, proceeded on our march and encamped at night in the wood.

Wednesday, Aug. 4th.—At 7 o'clock in the morning the General beat, struck our tents, proceeded on our march and encamped at night at Venderlips[47] Plantation. This day's march was very fatiguing. Our regiment was on the rear guard, the road very mountainous and difficult. We had the care of all the pack horses and cattle, which was very troublesome.

Thursday, Aug. 5th.—About 10 o'clock decamped, proceeded on our march and arrived at Wyalusing[48] and encamped there.

Friday, Aug. 6th.—Laid still at Wyalusing for refreshment.

---

a beautiful cascade comes rushing down from the mountain called Falling Springs. It proceeds from several never-failing springs on the summit. Hubley says, "to attempt a description of it would be almost presumption. Let this short account thereof suffice. The first or upper fall thereof is nearly ninety feet perpendicular, pouring from a solid rock, ushering forth a most beautiful echo, and is received by a cleft of rocks, considerably more projected than the former, from whence it rolls gradually and falls into the Susquehanna."

46. Quailutimack, seven miles from Lackawanna, signifying *"we came unawares upon them."* A place between the steep mountain and the river, said to have been the place of an Indian battle. The camp was on a "spot of ground situated on the river open and clear, containing about twelve hundred acres, soil very rich, timber fine, grass in abundance, and contains several springs."—*Hubley's Journal.*

47. Van der Lippe's.—Now Black Walnut in the town of Meshoppen, Wyoming County. So called from a Tory of that name, who was the first settler, above the Lackawanna, who previous to this time had abandoned the valley, and afterward died in Canada. During this day's march the army passed over Indian Hill, where Colonel Hartley had a battle with the Indians the previous year.

48. Wyalusing. At present Wyalusing in Bradford County.—"Passing up the river we came to a place called by the Indians Gohontoto. Here they tell us was in early times an Indian town, traces of which are still noticeable, e.g., corn pits, &c., inhabited by a distinct nation (neither Aquinoschioni, *i.e.*, Iroquois, nor Delawares) who spoke a peculiar language and were called Tehotitachsae; against these the Five Nations warred, and rooted them out. The Cayugas for a time held a number of them, but the nation and their language are now exterminated and extinct. This war, said the Indian, fell in the time when the Indians fought in battle with *bows and arrows* before they had guns and rifles."—*Cammerhoff & Zeisberger's Journal,* 1750. This was also the seat of the Moravian mission of Friedenshtuten, established in 1765, abandoned in 1772. This was about a mile below, (cont. next page),

Saturday, Aug. 7th.—Laid still on account of rainy weather.

Sunday, August 8th.[49]—At six o'clock in the morning struck camp, moved from Wyalusing and encamped at evening at a place called Standing Stone.[50]

Monday, Aug. 9th.—At six o'clock in the morning struck our tents, proceeded on our march and arrived at Sheshehung flats[51] and encamped there.

Tuesday, Aug. 10th.—Laid still at the Flats.

Wednesday, Aug. 11th.—At 6 o'clock in the morning struck tent, marched at 7 o'clock for Tyuga, (see note following). Our regiment and the 2nd New Jersey regiment was ordered to cross the river at our encampment and proceed up the river on the opposite side, to take possession of the ground at Tyuga to cover the fording place for the army and horses to cross the river, arrived at Tyuga about 11 o'clock in the morning.[52]

Wyalusing Creek, on the farms now occupied by G.H. Wells and J.B. Stafford. Rogers devotes several pages to a description of this town.

49. Newtychanning.—This day Colonel Proctor destroyed the first Indian town, named Newtychanning, containing about twenty houses, located on the west side of the Susquehanna, on the north side of Sugar Creek near North Towanda. Sullivan says it contained twenty-two houses; Canfield, that it was built the preceding year and contained from fifteen to twenty houses. This was near the site of Oscalui, of a previous date, and the same site called Ogehage, on Captain Hendricksen's map of 1616, and was then one of the towns of the Carantouannais, an Iroquois tribe destroyed or driven out by the Five Nations previous to 1650.

50. Standing Stone.—A large and long rock, on the west side of the river, said to have been detached from its bed on the mountain and taking a downward course, displacing all obstacles, took a final leap from the top of the precipice, and landed in a vertical position in the water near the shore, and remains a standing stone. The main army encamped directly opposite this, on Standing Stone flats; Hand's brigade on Wysox Creek three miles above.

51. Sheshequin Flats.—On site of present Sheshequin in Bradford County, on the opposite side of the river on site of present Ulster, was the Indian village of Sheshequin, six miles below Tioga. Cash's creek divided the town into two parts, the north side being heathen, those on the south Moravian Christians. About 1772 the latter removed six miles north and founded a new town, afterward known as Queen Esther's Town. Sheshequin was destroyed by Colonel Hartley in 1778.

52 Break-Neck Hill.—The army passed this day Break-Neck Hill, nearly opposite North Towanda. "This mountain derives its name from the great height of the difficult and narrow passage not more than a foot wide, and remarkable precipice which is immediately perpendicular, and not less than one hundred and eighty feet deep. One misstep must inevitably carry you from top to bottom without the least hope or chance of recovery."—*Hubley's Journal.* "This day (continued next page),

At night General Sullivan sent off a small scout[53] to discover Shemung[54] (of one captain and seven men,) which lay about twelve miles up the Tiyuga branch.

Note.—Tioga, the name given by the Iroquois to the wedge of land lying between the Chemung River and north branch of the Susquehanna; from *Teyaogen*, an interval, or anything between two other things [Bruyas, Agniers Racines]. *Teiohogen*, the forks of a river (Gallatin's vocabulary 387). This has from time immemorial been one of the most important strategical points of the country of the Five Nations. Zeisberger passed through here in 1750 and says that:

> . . . .at Tioga or *the gate*, Six Nations Indians were stationed for the purpose of ascertaining the character of all persons who crossed over into their country, and that whoever entered their territory by any other way than through the gate, or by way of the Mohawk, was suspected by them of evil purpose and treated as a spy or enemy.

An Indian town of Tioga near the point, destroyed by Colonel Hartley in 1778.

The earliest known account of the place is found in Champlain, who sent out one of his interpreters, named Stephen Brulé, in 1615, to arrange with the Carantouannais for a force of five hundred warriors, to co-operate with him in an attack on the Onondaga stronghold, then located on the town of Fenner, Madison Co., N.Y. Brulé with a small party of Hurons passed through the country of the Five Nations, to the great town of Carantouan, containing more than eight hundred warriors, then located on the so-called Spanish Hill near Waverly. Brulé

marched on the side of a mountain about three hundred feet from the bottom in a narrow path, where if we were to step one foot to our left we would be gone, and on our right the mountain was about four hundred feet high. N.B.—Three cows fell down and broke every bone in their bodies."—*Shute's Journal.*

53. Captain Cummings of the 3rd N.J., Lieutenant Jenkins, Captain Franklin and five others.

54. Chemung—An Indian town of fifty or sixty houses, occupied in 1779, located on the left bank of the Chemung River, three miles above the present village of Chemung, in Chemung County, destroyed by General Sullivan Aug. 13th, 1779. Old Chemung.—an Indian town partially abandoned in 1779, located on the left bank of the Chemung River, half a mile above the present village of Chemung, in Chemung County. A few houses burned Aug. 13th, 1779

returned to Carantouan after the expedition, and the next year, 1616, went down the Susquehanna to the sea "where he found many nations that are powerful and warlike."

The three Dutchmen mentioned in the note on Wyoming passed down the Susquehanna Branch and were probably the first white men who ever saw that river; Brulé, the first that ever saw the Chemung.

Aug. 12.—The scout returned with news that the enemy seemed to be in great confusion and seemed to be moving off. The general left a guard at Tiyuga sufficient to guard the camp and marched with the rest of the army under cover of the night for Shemung, marched all night, the weather very dark, and nothing but an Indian path through the wood made it difficult.[55]

Friday, Aug. 13th.—About six o'clock in the morning we arrived at Shemung and found the enemy had left the town. On our approach we burnt the town, destroyed the corn, &c., and returned to Tiyuga. A small party of the Indians who had concealed themselves in the wood, fired on a small party of General Hand's brigade, killed six men and wounded two without loss on their side.[56] A party of General Poor's brigade was destroying corn, were fired upon by the enemy, killed one and wounded one.

Saturday, Aug. 14th.—Laid at Tiyuga waiting for the arrival of General Clinton's brigade, who came down the Susquehanna from the

---

55. This night's march was very tedious. The path followed the north bank of the Chemung, passing the first narrows, near present Waverly, and the second along the steep hillsides and precipices west of present Chemung. At these points there was scarcely room for two to walk abreast, and a single misstep would insure a landing on the rocks a hundred feet below. It was daylight when the troops reached the second narrows, but a dense fog prevailed, under the cover of which they advanced, and found the town abandoned.

56. Chemung Ambuscade.—On the failure to surprise the Indians in their village, General Hand pursued them up the river. About a mile above New Chemung, the trail passed obliquely over a hill known locally as the Hog Back, near the present residence of Doctor Everett, about two and a half miles below the monument on Sullivan Hill. Colonel Hubley's regiment was in front, with Captain Bush's company of forty men on the right acting as flankers, with the two Independent Companies in the rear. The head of the column appears to have been somewhat in advance of the flankers and when near the summit of the hill, received a fire from the enemy in ambush, at short range. Six were killed and nine wounded, among the latter Captain Franklin, Captain Carbury and Adjutant Huston, all of Colonel Hubley's regiment. The enemy at once retreated to the thicket north of the hill.

Mohawk River. A large detachment from the army was ordered up to join him, (see note following). The remainder of the army were employed in building a garrison at Tiyuga.[57] On the 22nd day of August we were joined by General Clinton's brigade.

Note.—The following extract from the *Journal of Major Norris*, describes the march of this detachment up the north side of the Susquehanna from Tioga to Union in the town of Union, Broome County, where they met General Clinton's brigade. For the march of Clinton down the Susquehanna see Beatty's *Journal*:

Aug. 15th.—Nine Hundred chosen men under the command of Brigadier General Poor are ordered to march tomorrow morning up the Susquehanna, to meet General Clinton, who is on his march to join Sullivan's army with his brigade and is in some danger of being attacked by the enemy before he can form a junction with our main army; This afternoon a small party of Indian's fired on some of our men who were without the guards after some horse's, and cattle, killed and sculped one man and wounded another, a party was sent out in pursuit of them but could not come up with them—

16th General Poor marched with his detachment at 10 o'clock a.m. proceeded in two collam's up the Suscuhannah River over very rough ground we incampt near the ruins of an old town called Macktowanuck the land near the river is very good—

17th We marched early this morning proceed twelve miles to Owagea an Indian town which was deserted last spring, after planting, About the town is many fruit trees and many plants, and herbs, that are common in our part of the country; hear is a learge body of clear intivale covered with grass, Our march today very survear and fatigueing especelly for the left collm (to which I belong) as we had to pass several steap hills and morasses.—

18th We proceeded fourteen miles to Choconant the remains

---

57. Fort Sullivan—near the centre of the present village (continued next page), of Athens, where the two rivers approach near each other. It was about one, hundred yards square, with a strong block house at each angle, two opposite ones resting on the banks of the rivers, and the two others about midway between. The curtains were made by setting logs endwise in the ground, the whole being surrounded by a ditch, making a work of ample strength. Colonel Shreve was left in command with a garrison of two hundred and fifty men beside the invalids, with two pieces of artillery.

of a learge Indian town which has been likewise abandoned this summer, here we found plenty of cucombar's, squashes, turnips &c. We found about twenty houses, which we burnt our days march has been more survear than yesterday, as we had bad hills and swamps, one swamp of about two miles so covered with large pines, standing and lying which appeared as though several haricanes had been busy among since which a tremendius groath of bushes About twenty feet high has sprung up so very thick as to render the passing through them impractible by any troops but such as nothing but death can stop—at sunset we were very agreeably alarmed by the report of a cannon up the river which was supposed to be General Clintons evening gun—

19th Our troops were put in motion very early this morning after marching about one mile General Poor received an exspress from General Clinton informing him that the latter exspected to be hear by 10 o'clock a.m. this day in consiquence of which we returned to our old incampment where General Clinton, Joined us at 10 o'clock with two thousand men—including officers, boatsman &c. he has two hundred and eight *beautoes* with provisions ammunition &c. after mutual congratulations and complements the whole proceeded down the river to Owagea and incampt this evening, the town of Owegea was made a burnfire of to grace our meating . . . . . .

Monday, August 23rd.—Laid still. Captain Kimble of Colonel Cilley's regiment, General Poor's brigade, was killed in his tent by accident with a gun being snapped by a soldier.

Tuesday, 24th August.—The disposition was made and everything got in readiness for marching. The army encamped that evening agreeable to the order of march,[58] myself being drafted on the right flank, which was commanded by Colonel Dubois.

Wednesday, 25th.—Laid still not being able to get ready to march on account of our pack horses.

---

58. The order of march was arranged to form a hollow square, General Hand's brigade in front; General Poor's on the right; General Maxwell's on the left; and General Clinton's in the rear. Within the square was Colonel Proctor's artillery, and eight lines of led pack horses, and the beef cattle. On the right of General Poor was a flanking division, and flank guard, of two hundred and fifty men under Colonel Dubois; and a like flanking division and guard, on the left of Maxwell, under command of Colonel Ogden. A strong advance guard of light infantry covered the front.

Thursday, 26th.—Struck tents at 1 o'clock and marched about three miles up the Tiyuga Branch and encamped.

Friday, August 27.—At 8 o'clock in the morning the General beat, struck tents at 9 o'clock marched off and encamped that night about three miles below Shemung by a large cornfield.[59]

Saturday, August 28th.—At 3 o'clock in the afternoon marched as far as Shemung and encamped.[60]

Sunday, 29th August.—At 8 o'clock in the morning the signal for march was given. We marched about four miles when our Light corps fell in with the enemy on the opposite side of a defile with some slight works thrown up in their front. The light troops exchanged some shots with them and amused them whilst Generals Clinton's and Poor's brigades with the right flank were ordered to file off by the right and gain the enemy's rear, which to effect, we had to ascend a very steep hill which the enemy had possessed themselves of. Whilst we were gaining the rear, Colonel Proctor with the artillery kept up a brisk fire on their works.

On our ascending the hill they began to attack us. Our men undauntedly pushed on and gained the hill. The enemy went off in confusion, left their dead on the ground.(see note following)—About sunset we encamped on the enemy's ground.[61] We had one major, one

---

59. Encamped on the site of Old Chemung, burned Aug. 13th. See note 54.

60. Encamped on the flats, near New Chemung, see note 54. The army passed a very difficult defile, known as the "Narrows" west of present Chemung; the artillery forded the river twice.

61. Four towns were destroyed in the vicinity of the battle field, *viz.*:

1st. Newtown, an Indian village of about twenty houses, occupied in 1779, located on the left bank of the Chemung River about five miles below Elmira, and a mile above the fortified position between Baldwin's creek and the river. It gave the name to the battle fought near it Aug. 29, 1779.

2nd. A small village north east of the battle field of Newtown on both sides of Baldwin's Creek, of twenty to thirty houses which had never been occupied, and were supposed to have been built for storing the crops grown in the vicinity. This was located at the point where General Poor commenced the ascent of the hill; and was destroyed by Clinton's brigade.

3rd. A small village near the angle in the works of the enemy on Baldwin's Creek, the timbers of which were used by them in the construction of the fortifications. One house in front of their works was occupied by the enemy as a block house during the engagement.

4th. "*Monday, Aug. 30*. . . . .Went up the river about two miles, then took up a long branch of the river (which runs near S. W.) one mile, burnt five houses and destroyed all the corn in our way."—*Beatty's Journal.*

captain and one lieutenant wounded. The captain and lieutenant died of their wounds, also a few men wounded[62]

Note.— The Battle of Newtown was fought on Sunday, Aug. 29, 1779, near the Indian village of the same name, on the left bank of the Chemung River six miles south east of Elmira. The enemy's force of British regulars, two battalions of Royal Greens, and Tories, were led by Colonel John Butler, with Captains Walter N. Butler and Macdonald as subordinates; the Indians by the great Mohawk Captain Thayendanegea, *alias* Joseph Brant, Butler being in chief command. The design of the enemy appears to have been primarily, an ambuscade. They had artfully concealed their works, and posted their forces in positions to attack simultaneously, both flanks, front, and rear; the position naturally strong, was admirably adapted to their purposes.

From Elmira, extending south easterly for several miles, is a mountainous ridge, running parallel with the river, something over six hundred feet in height near the Indian village, but gradually melting away to the level of the plain where it terminates about a mile below; on this south eastern slope was the Battle of Newtown. To the north and east of this ridge is a similar one, which also terminates near the battle field, and between them is a considerable stream, which, running nearly parallel with the river in its general course, enters the Chemung a mile and a quarter below.

The river here sweeps around in a graceful curve, making a full semi-circle, enclosing several hundred acres of rich bottom lands, on which were the Indian cornfields; the Wellsburg north and south road dividing it into two nearly equal parts. Rising abruptly from this plain is a sharp, narrow ridge, known locally as the Hog Back, this extends from the river across the plain nearly to the creek, a distance of about a third of a mile. The crest of this ridge was occupied by the enemy in force, protected by rude log breast works and rifle pits, which extended to the eastern extremity, and from thence turning north,

---

62. The loss of our army is variously given in different accounts of the action. Major Livermore (*Journal Aug. 29*) says that "but four or five" were killed and three officers and about "thirty others" were wounded. Lieutenant Barton (Journal) that two or three of ours were killed and "thirty-four or five wounded." General Sullivan, in a despatch written the next day after the fight, makes the entire loss *three* killed and thirty nine wounded.

connected with the steep banks of the creek above. The lines to be defended were these two sides of a triangle, their right resting on the river, their left on the mountain, the path of the army passing between the two lines, along which was also the enemy's line of retreat.

From the angle in the works a thin line extended to the mountain, on which was a body of the enemy and also another small body on the mountain to the east. The results at Chemung a few days previous, led the enemy to hope that a like blunder might be repeated, and that Wyoming and Minnisinks were to be re-enacted. Presuming that the army, after crossing the creek, would follow the Indian trail without discovering their works, they flattered themselves that an unexpected fire on the exposed flanks would create great confusion, which if augmented by simultaneous attacks in front and rear by the forces in that quarter, might result in a panic, and a possible stampede of the pack horses and cattle, which would be quite as disastrous as the defeat of the army.

But three companies of Morgan's riflemen, the pride of Washington, were in the advance; these veterans of a hundred battles were in no way inferior to the enemy in Indian craft; the works and position of the enemy were discovered when afar off, and this ingenious device of drawing our forces into an ambuscade was frustrated. The ambuscade failing, the alternative was presented of forcing a direct attack in front, under great disadvantage, or of a flanking movement, over very difficult ground, where nearly the entire force of the enemy could be brought to bear on the attacking force at any point on interior lines, possibly in time to repulse one division of the army before the other could come to its relief.

The attack in front was invited by repeated sorties of a body of about four hundred of the enemy, who would deliver their fire, and immediately retreat to their works. After three hours of skirmishing, deliberation, and reconnoitring, General Sullivan determined to divide his force, turn the enemy's left, and attack simultaneously in front and flank.

The artillery was posted on a rising ground, three hundred yards from the enemy, in position to enfilade the main line of their works, and sweep the ground in the rear, General Hand was to support the artillery, the left flanking division to threaten the enemy's right, and General Maxwell's brigade to be held in reserve. General Poor's brigade of four regiments, the right flanking division, and the three companies of riflemen, were to make a circuit of about two miles and turn the enemy's left and attack in flank and rear, to be supported by General Clinton's brigade of four regiments following as a second line.

One hour was allowed for this movement, at the expiration of which, the artillery was to open, to be followed by a general assault of the two divisions. Poor almost immediately after commencing his march, found himself involved in a thicket of underbrush, almost impenetrable, but after great difficulty reached the foot of the hill on which the enemy was posted, just at the moment the artillery fire commenced. Forming his line of battle with Lieutenant Colonel Reid's 2nd N.H. on the extreme left, next to him Lieutenant Colonel Dearborn's 2nd N.H., then Alden's 6th Mass., and Colonel Cilley's 1st N.H. on the extreme right.

To the right of the brigade was the right flanking division of two hundred and fifty men under Colonel Dubois, the whole preceded by three companies of riflemen under Major Parr. General Clinton's brigade formed line of battle with Colonel Gansevoort's 3rd N.Y. on the left, next Dubois 5th N.Y., then Livingston's 4th N.Y., with Van Courtlandt's 2nd N.Y. on the extreme right, following in the rear of the first line. Poor when about half way up the hill encountered the enemy, but not in sufficient force to materially check the advance of the flanking division, or the regiments on his right; on reaching the summit of the hill, these rapidly pushed forward to seize the defile near the river, a short distance above Newtown, which was the only avenue of escape for the enemy.

Almost at the commencement of the cannonade, the main force of the enemy adroitly abandoned their works without being discovered, and precipitated themselves on Colonel Reid's regiment in greatly superior numbers. They swarmed about him in a semi-circle, and for a few moments made the forest ring with their exultant shouts, but for a few minutes only; for Colonel Dearborn having reached the summit of the hill, and missing Colonel Reid on his left, on his own responsibility, faced his regiment to the rear and moved to his assistance. At the same moment the two regiments on the left of Clinton's brigade by a left oblique movement, came up from the rear to Reid's support, and the enemy soon found themselves dangerously threatened.

The conflict was short, sharp and decisive, and the war whoop soon gave place to the retreat halloo. Poor with the remainder of his brigade, followed by the two regiments on the right of Clinton, had pushed rapidly for the defile. In the meantime Hand had advanced in front, and the left flanking division under Colonel Ogden had worked its way along the river on the enemy's flank, when, the enemy admirably commanded, and wisely discreet, sounded the signal for retreat just in time to escape. A British account says:

> In this action Colonel Butler and all his people was surrounded, and very near being taken prisoners. On the same day a few miles from this he attempted again to stop them, but in vain. The colonel lost four rangers killed, two taken prisoners and seven wounded.

Twelve Indians were found dead on the field, the number of wounded unknown. The enemy were pursued for two or three miles above Newtown by the light troops, where Salmon says they made another stand, which appears to be confirmed by the account above quoted, but no details are given, and the matter is not alluded to in General Sullivan's official report. The loss in killed according to the Indian official account, found four days after, near Catharine's town is as follows:

> *Sept. 3rd.*—This day found a tree marked 1779, Thandagana, the English of which is Brant, twelve men marked on it with arrows pierced through them, signifying the number they had lost in the action of the 29th *ultimo*. A small tree was twisted round like a rope and bent down which signified that if we drove and distressed them, yet we would not conquer them.

August 30.—Remained on the ground of yesterday. The greatest part of the army were employed in destroying corn which was in great abundance.

Tuesday, 31st August.—At 9 o'clock in the morning marched off; marched ten miles above Newtown and encamped on a large pine plain, forming a square with our camp to secure our pack horses and cattle.

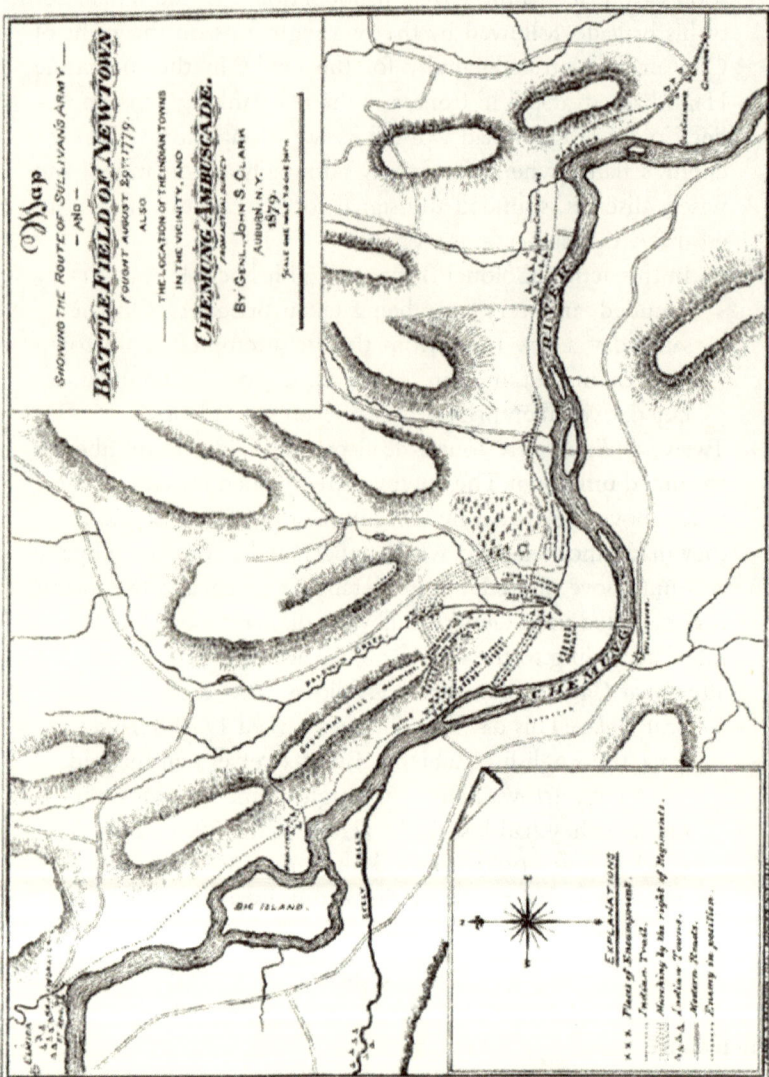

Map
— AND —
SHOWING THE ROUTE OF SULLIVAN'S ARMY
BATTLE FIELD OF NEWTOWN
FOUGHT AUGUST 29TH, 1779.
ALSO
THE LOCATION OF THE INDIAN TOWNS
IN THE VICINITY, AND
CHEMUNG AMBUSCADE.
By GENL. JOHN S. CLARK,
AUBURN, N.Y.
1879.

EXPLANATIONS.
Places of Encampment.
Indian Trail.
Marching by the right of Regiments.
Indian Towns.
Modern Roads.
Enemy in position.

BIG ISLAND.

Note.—During the march this day two towns were burned, *viz.*:

Middletown.—A small Indian town mentioned in several journals as lying between Newtown and Kanawlohalla, on the north side of the river, consisting of eight houses, destroyed Aug. 31 by the army while on the march.

Kanawlohalla.—Signifying *a head on a pole*, located on the present site of Elmira, destroyed by Sullivan's army Aug. 31. In some journals this town is called Newtown, and the one near the battle field Lower Newtown, but a majority designate it by its Indian name, which, according to Mr. Maxwell should be spelled Canaweola, as pronounced by Red Jacket, and who also gave the signification, and the legend connected with it.

Colonel Dayton with the 3rd N.J. regiment and a detachment of riflemen were detached here and sent up the river in pursuit of the enemy, whom the advanced guard saw escaping in their canoes. He failed to overtake them, but found an Indian village at or near present Big Flats, which he destroyed. He encamped here for the night and rejoined the main army the next morning, by a march north-east through the valley, where the main body were encamped near present Horse Heads.

Wednesday, Sept. 1st.—The signal gun fired at 8 o'clock in the morning. We marched at half past nine, marched about six miles through a flat level road at the end of which we entered a dark pine swamp, which continued four miles with almost impassable hills and valleys and arrived at 11 o'clock at night at Catharine's town.

Note.—Catharine's Town—*She-o-qua-ga.*—An Indian village located on the high ground a little south of the present village of Havana. The town was on both sides of the inlet and about three miles from the head of the lake. This was the residence of the famous Catharine Montour, by many writers incorrectly confounded with Madame Montour, and by others with Queen Esther, of Wyoming notoriety.

Madame Montour, a noted personage in the Colonial history of Pennsylvania, resided at one time at the present site of Montoursville, in Pennsylvania, on the west branch of the Susquehanna, afterwards on an island near Shamokin; and about 1749, when very aged and blind, removed to the vicinity of Lake Erie, where she probably died previous to 1752. She had several sons and one daughter, all distinguished characters in Pennsylvania annals.

Queen Esther, notorious as the "fiend of Wyoming," "who followed in the train of the victorious army, ransacking the heaps of slain, and with arms covered with gore barbarously murdering the wounded who in vain supplicated for their lives." She was living at Sheshequin six miles below Tioga point in 1772, and removed about that date six miles north, and founded a new town, afterward known as Queen Esther's town; this was afterward destroyed by Colonel Hartley in 1778, when she probably removed to Chemung. She had a sister Mary, and one son, who lost his life a short time previous to the massacre of Wyoming, which was probably the exciting cause of her fury at that place. She afterward settled on the point south of Union Springs, in Cayuga County, and died there of old age.

Catharine Montour was young enough to be the granddaughter of Madame Montour. At the time of Sullivan's campaign and for some years previous she had resided at her village near present Havana. She had two sons, Roland and John, and a daughter Belle. Her sons were conspicuous characters at Cherry Valley, Wyoming and in Sullivan's campaign, where John was wounded in the battle of Newtown. Roland married the daughter of Siangorochti, the chief *sachem* of the Senecas; both sons were known as captains in the many Indian raids against the border settlements. Catharine's reputed husband was Edward Pollard, a sutler at Fort Niagara, who was also the father of the famous Seneca warrior, Captain Pollard, by another Indian wife. There was at this time another Captain John Montour near Fort Pitt, who accompanied Colonel Brodhead in his expedition up the Allegany, who was loyal to the American cause throughout the war. In this expedition of Colonel Brodhead, the husband of Belle Montour was killed.

Thursday, 2nd.—Laid still. Our line of march being confused by the badness of the road the day before.

Friday, Sept 3rd.—The signal gun fired at 7 o'clock, the army marched off at 8 o'clock, marched about twelve miles and encamped in the wood on the east side of the Seneca Lake.[63] The land good and well timbered.

---

63. Peach Orchard, a small Indian town, was destroyed here, August 3rd, on the point, called Apple-tree town in Nukerck's *Journal*. Jenkins says "the army encamped about 4 in the afternoon near a small Indian settlement," &c.

Saturday, ye 4th Sept.—The General beat at 9 o'clock in the morning. The army marched at 10 o'clock, marched four miles and halted.[64]

Sunday ye 5th.—The General beat at half past 9 o'clock, the army marched at 10 o'clock and encamped in a town called Candaya,[65] or Appletown.

Monday, Sept 6th.—At two o'clock in the afternoon left Appletown and marched about three miles and encamped in the wood.[66]

Tuesday ye 7th.—At 8 o'clock in the morning struck tents, marched off and crossed the outlet of the Ceneca Lake, where we expected to meet some opposition, but the enemy had left the town. We entered it, found a white child[67] in the town, supposed to be about four years old, it was supposed they had taken away from the frontiers, where they had destroyed and burnt. The Ceneca Lake is supposed to be

---

64. Condawhaw.—An Indian town occupied in 1779, located on the east side of Seneca Lake on the present site of North Hector, was so called in 1778 by Luke Swetland, who passed through it while on his way to Kendaia. It was burned by the army Sept. 4, 1779. It is called Apple Town in William Barton's *Journal*.

65. Kendaia, a town containing about twenty houses, located on lot 79 Romulus, on the east side of Seneca Lake, on land now owned by Edward Van Vliet. It was about half a mile from the lake, on both sides of a small stream. Luke Swetland resided here for a year as a prisoner, until rescued by the army. Several journals give interesting accounts of this town, and especially of the Indian tombs, which appear to have been arranged with more than ordinary care. It was the custom on the death of distinguished personages to paint on their monumental posts a record of important events relating to the history of the deceased person. The fact that these tombs were different in construction and style of ornamentation from others, suggests the idea that they were a remnant of some subjugated tribe, differing in mode of burial from the Iroquois. A noted Seneca warrior named Kendaia was conspicuous at the siege of Ft. Niagara in 1759.

66. Lieutenant Hardenbergh mentions the fact of being "drafted on the right flank, which was commanded by Colonel Dubois." He was probably one of the one hundred men drafted from the line, as part of the right flanking division, and consequently would be on the extreme right of the army while *en route*. The centre line of the army was the regular Indian trail, which was opened to a sufficient width for the passage of the artillery. Along Seneca Lake, the present lake road follows substantially on the line of the trail. At this point, Beatty says "we encamped close along the edge of the lake, and opposite to us on the west side of the lake, we could perceive a small Indian town." See note 68, Gothseungquean.

67. This child was tenderly cared for, adopted by Captain Machin, an officer in the artillery, and christened Thomas Machin. After the return of the army it was placed in a family near Kingston, N.Y., where it died some two years after of small pox. No clue was ever obtained as to its parentage.

thirty-six miles in length from south to north. The land along the east side appears to be a rich soil and well timbered. At the north end is the outlet which is a continual stream and considerable large. About three miles and a half from the outlet is the town Cannadasago or Ceneca Castle.[68]

Wednesday ye 8th Sept.—Laid still at Cannadasago.

Thursday ye 9th.—Marched from Cannadasago about eight miles and encamped in the wood[69]

Friday 10th.—At 7 o'clock marched off about seven miles and crossed the outlet of a small lake, a few miles from which stood a town called Canandagui,[70] about fifteen and a half miles from Ceneca Castle, which we entered, and encamped at 3 o'clock, about a mile north of the town in a large cornfield.

Saturday ye 11th Sept.—Struck our tents at 9 o'clock and marched about nine miles through an open country, halted at 11 o'clock for refreshment, moved at one o'clock, and arrived at a small town called Honyuga.[71] At this town we left a small garrison of one captain, one

68. Kanadaseaga, the *grand village*, so called from being the residence of the chief *sachem* of the Senecas, located one and a half miles north-west of present village of Geneva on both sides of Kanadaseaga Creek. This was the capital of the Seneca nation and contained about sixty well built houses. A stockade fort was built here in 1756 by Sir William Johnson, the remains of which were in existence in 1779 Rev. Samuel Kirkland was a missionary here in 1764-6. Was destroyed Sept. 9. Butler's Buildings.—A small village called Butler's Buildings was found on the shore of the lake, near present canal bridge, in the village of Geneva. Gothseungquean, also called *Shenanwaga* and many other dialectical variations, an important town, was also destroyed Sept. 8, by a detachment of riflemen under Major Parr. The name is perpetuated in Kershong Creek, on which it was situated, on Seneca Lake, seven miles south of Geneva. It contained twenty houses.

69. From Kanadaseaga the route was first south west for about two miles to the line of the present turnpike, and thence nearly due west along the line of the turnpike to Canandaigua Lake. Beatty mentions an ancient stockade fort between Kanadaseaga and Canandaigua. This was on Flint Creek on lot 92 in N.W. corner of the town of Seneca. The encampment was on Flint Creek.

70. Kanandaigua, an Indian town of twenty-three large houses mostly framed, located about a mile from the lake shore, in west part of present village of Canandaigua. The cornfields, which were very extensive, were located on the ridge north of the town. The usual variety and quantity of fruit trees were found here, all of which were destroyed. From Kanandaigua the route of the army was nearly south west, substantially on the line of the present road through Bristol to the foot of Honeoye Lake, a distance of sixteen miles, to the next village of Hanneyaye.

71. Hanneyaye, an Indian town occupied in 1779, located at the foot of Honeoye Lake, about half a mile east of the outlet, and south (continued next page),

lieutenant and fifty men, exclusive of invalids, with some flour, horses and cattle.

Sunday 12th.—Left Haunyuga at 12 o'clock, marched about 11 miles and encamped in the wood.[72]

Monday, 13th.—At five o'clock in the morning marched about two miles to a small town called Adjutoa, from this place the General sent out a scout of one sub. and nineteen men to reconnoitre a town that was in front. On his return he was attacked by about 100 Indians and were all killed but two men who had the good fortune to make their escape. The army remained in town till about 12 o'clock. Some were employed in destroying corn and some in building a bridge (across a mirey swamp and creek) for the artillery to pass. While we were so employed the surveyor[73] had advanced a little in front of the advanced guard, was fired upon by the Indians and had one of his party wounded.[74] At 12 o'clock we left the town, and arrived at a town called Cassawauloughly, seven miles from Adjutoa, which we entered at sunset.[75]

---

of Mill Creek. It contained about twenty houses, one of which was occupied as a fort under command of Captain Cummings of the 2nd N.J. regiment. Beatty gives the following description of the work which he says was occupied by three hundred men in all: "They was encamped round the house where we had left our stores, and the camp was abbateed in, and round the house they had made a small fort of kegs, and bags of flour, and had three pieces of artillery in it, and the house they had made full of loop holes, so as to fight out of it in case of necessity, and upon the whole I think they was very safe."

72. On leaving Hanneyaye the army forded the outlet near the lake, and taking a west course, nearly on the line of the present east and west road leading west from present village of Honeoye, to the summit of the dividing ridge, and thence in a south west course, crossing the outlet of Hemlock lake at its foot, and continuing over the hill on same course to present Foot's Corners, in the town of Conesus, where the army encamped on level ground two miles north of the Indian town Adjutoa or Kanaghsaws.

73. Captain Benjamin Lodge, with a party of assistants accompanied the army and with chain and compass surveyed the entire route of the army from Easton to the great Genesee town. On the return march he accompanied Colonel Butler's expedition through the Cayuga country.

74. Corporal Calhawn, a volunteer, died the next day.

75. Chenussio.—This town, though not in existence at the time of Sullivan's campaign, is intimately connected with its history. It was located on the site of ancient Williamsburg, near the confluence of the Canaseraga and the Genesee, on the east side of the latter river. It appears on the Guy Johnson map of 1771 as Chenussio, on the Pouchot map of 1758 as Connecchio, in both cases at the point described and where Mary Jennison's narrative says it was in her day. In 1750 it was visited by Cammerhoff and Zeisberger, two Moravian (continued over page),

Map
SHOWING THE ROUTE OF
SULLIVAN'S ARMY
AND
GROVELAND AMBUSCADE.
SEPTEMBER 13TH, 1779.
WITH PLACES OF ENCAMPMENT AND POSITION OF
INDIAN TOWNS IN THE VICINITY.
FROM — ACTUAL SURVEY
BY GEN'L JOHN S. CLARK.
AUBURN, N.Y.
1879.

EXPLANATIONS:
Place of Encampment.
Indian Trail.
Marching marching in Column.
Indian Towns.
Modern Towns.
Modern Roads.
Road where Smiths Indians were buried.
Swamp on Inundation.

Notes:

Kanaghsaws, or Adjutoa according to some journals, an Indian town of eighteen houses, located about a mile north west of Conesus Centre, on the north and south road that passes through the McMillen farm. Between the town and the lake on Henderson's Flats were the cornfields. The village appears to have occupied the grounds in the vicinity of the McMillen residence, and extended north across the creek, and southward to the plateau now covered by an orchard which was probably an ancient palisaded site of the town. The main body of the army encamped on the night of the 12th nearly two miles north on the flats, south-west of Foot's Corners.

A local tradition exists that Hand with the light troops followed the road through Union Corners and encamped on the L.B. Richardson farm, south west of Conesus Centre at the False Faces, but nothing of the kind is found in any of the journals, and is probably incorrect. George Grant says a fine stream of water ran through the town, and that "Captain Sunfish, a negro, resided here, a very bold, enterprising fellow, who commanded the town." Several journals mention the fact that Big Tree, a noted Indian warrior, also made this his home.

President Dwight describes him as a man of lofty character and dignified deportment, and that he had strenuously urged his countrymen to observe strict neutrality, but without success. The chieftain stood on an elevated spot and saw his own possessions destroyed. "You see how the Americans treat their friends," said some of those around him, favourable to Great

missionaries, who called it Connesschio and describe it as then containing forty houses. All of these names are dialectical and orthographical variations of the modern word Genesee, signifying *the beautiful valley*. Gaustarax, a celebrated Seneca Chief, was for many years a leading spirit of this town, and during the French and Indian war, being thoroughly in the interests of the French, it required all the diplomatic ability of Sir William Johnson, and the influence of the other nations of the league, to neutralize his efforts. It was in existence as early as 1750, and as late as 1770, but in 1768 it had ceased to be the western door, which honour was then held by the great town of Chenandoanes, on the west side of the river. At the time of Sullivan's campaign it had ceased to exist or had dwindled into an insignificance unworthy of mention. This was the town that Boyd was sent to reconnoitre, and which Major Norris says the General expected to find on the east side of the river and two miles north of Gathtsegwarohare. This is the town also, that writers confound with the great town west of the river, and which so perplexed General Sullivan in his examination of the maps.

Britain. "What I see," calmly replied the chief, "is only the common fortune of war. It cannot be supposed that the Americans can distinguish my property from yours, who are their enemies." The army was engaged until near noon in destroying the crops and re-building the bridge which had been destroyed by the enemy.

Groveland Ambuscade.—This, one of the most important matters connected with Sullivan's campaign, has, for a hundred years, remained a stumbling block and mystery to historians. This has arisen in part from erroneous views as to the location of Gathtsegwarohare and the trails, but mainly from the mistaken idea that Boyd's party was the force against which the efforts of the enemy were originally directed, rather than that it was a formidable attempt to ambuscade the main army.

From Kanaghsaws the trail led south westerly across the low grounds following the line of the present road near the inlet, and crossing it at, or very near the site of the present bridge, about three-fourths of a mile from the head of the lake. North of the bridge, the banks of the inlet are low and marshy, in many places impassable for infantry, and at all points impassable for artillery and pack horses; while south of the bridge, is a wet swamp almost impenetrable from the thick growth of underbrush, west of the lake and Inlet is a steep hillside, the face of which, cut up by numerous ravines, is so steep that with considerable difficulty an army could march directly up it.

The trail after leaving the bridge probably continued south westerly up the hill obliquely, nearly on the line of the present highway to the summit of the bluff, and thence turning northwest followed along the heads of the ravines for a mile and thence directly west to Gathtsegwarohare. Directly west of the bridge, between two very deep ravines, is a space nearly half a mile in width, which continues up the hill on very favourable ground for the advance of the army. It appears to be the only point where it could advance in the order of march laid down, which would require a space of nearly a half a mile in width for the several columns.

After the Battle of Newtown, Butler and Brant with their demoralized forces, sullenly retired, powerless to prevent the advance of the devastating army. Butler had reached the last Indian village of Canawaugas, located on the west side of the

Genesee, twelve miles north of the Great Genesee Castle. Here he received reinforcements of regulars from Niagara, and determined to make one more effort against the invaders. Gathering all his available forces of regulars, Tories, and Indians, he left Canawaugas on the morning of the 12th of September, and probably reached the position on the hill west of Kanaghsaws, on the evening of the same day. Here they posted themselves north of the trail, at the heads of the ravines about three-fourths of a mile west of the bridge, and a mile and a half from Kanaghsaws.

This was a most admirable position for an ambuscade, and in many essential particulars of topography and fact, bears a striking resemblance to the fatal ground where Braddock so ingloriously sacrificed his army; and had Sullivan advanced in the same blundering manner, he too, might have met with an equally disastrous defeat. The plan appears to have been, to attack a portion of the army after it had crossed the bridge, or to ambuscade the head of the column while ascending the hill; but whatever may have been the original design, it was completely frustrated by the fortunate movements of the unfortunate Boyd.

It will be remembered that the army went into camp on the flats near Foot's Corners two miles north of the village of Kanaghsaws. Boyd and his party left camp at 11 o'clock at night, passed through the abandoned Kanaghsaws, and from thence pursued the direct trail which led south westerly up the hill to Gathtsegwarohare. In the darkness of the night, he passed Butler's right flank, neither party being conscious of the presence of the other, and reached Gathtsegwarohare, which the inhabitants had abandoned early in the morning, without encountering any difficulty.

On the morning of the 13th Sullivan advanced to Kanaghsaws, and finding that the enemy had destroyed the bridge over the inlet, he detailed a portion of the army to aid the pioneers in its reconstruction, and to repair the roadway over the low grounds leading to it. All of this was directly under the eye of Butler, who, according to a British account, "lay undiscovered though only a musket shot from the rebels, and even within sight." On reaching the town Boyd halted his forces at the suburbs, himself and one of his men reconnoitred the place, then rejoined the party and concealed themselves in the woods near the town. He sent back two of his men to report to General Sullivan, and awaited the light of the day whose morning was just breaking. These two men got through safely and reported.

About daybreak four Indians were seen to enter the town by Boyd, one of whom was killed, another wounded, the rest escaped. Boyd then immediately set out to return, expecting to meet the army on the march, and when about half way, despatched two more men to inform the general of his intention to remain "on the path" and await the coming of the army. These men soon encountered five Indians, and returned; the entire party then resumed the march, following and firing on the retreating Indians, who lured them directly into the lines of the enemy.

Colonel Butler hearing the firing on his right and rear imagined he was discovered, and that instead of ambuscading the rebels, he was himself to be surprised by this unexpected attack in the rear. No evidence whatever has appeared to confirm the conjecture, that Boyd's presence was either known or suspected in that quarter, by Butler, or any portion of his force, until discovered by the five retreating Indians, and to them, only by accident; but when discovered with true aboriginal cunning they allured their unsuspecting victims to the fatal embrace of the enemy, who came there to surprise an army, but were prevented by the blundering of a scout.

A few of Boyd's party who were acting as flankers escaped, five or six fell near the trail and were found when the army advanced, the remainder retreated a short distance north to a clump of trees, where their bodies were found all near together, and where all the bodies were buried on the return march of the army on the 16th. During the construction of the bridge a guard had been established west of the inlet, and Captain Lodge with his party engaged in making their surveys, had advanced some distance up the hill; the bridge was about completed when the fugitive flankers came rushing down the hill pursued by small parties of the enemy.

Hand's brigade immediately advanced up the hill to the position occupied by the enemy in the morning, where he found the packs of the enemy in the position they had left a few minutes previous. He remained here in line of battle until the army had crossed, and formed for the advance up the hill.

Gathtsegwarohare, so called by Nukerck; *Gaghegwalahale* by Dearborn; *Cassawauloughly* by Hardenburgh, was seven miles directly west of Kanaghsaws, on the east side of Canaseraga Creek about two miles above its confluence with the Genesee River. Here is a beautiful plateau of about six acres, admirably adapted for an Indian town, at present occupied by the house and surrounding grounds of the widely known "Hermitage," the ancestral home of the Carolls. The town contained twenty-five houses, mostly new, and appears to have been located on both sides of the stream north of the Caroll mansion.

The tribe residing here called Squa-tche-gas by Sullivan; by the Onondagas Tchoueragak, signifying wild cats; by Cusic Squaki-hows, and by others Kah-kwas, were the same that afterward settled at Squakie-Hill, to whom was reserved the two square miles in the Big Tree Treaty of 1797. They were a remnant of one of the tribes of the historic Eries, who occupied the territory to the south and east of Lake Erie whose blood, language, and league did not differ materially from the Iroquois Five Nations.

After a terrible conflict, and many bloody battles the Eries were finally overthrown about the year 1655, and a remnant incorporated with the league. They were permitted to live by themselves, to have a separate council fire and keep up a show of tribal rites, but were really vassals to do the bidding of their masters. Boyd and his party reached this town about at the break of day on the morning of the 13th, and found it abandoned. He sent two of his men to report to General Sullivan and concealed his force in the adjacent woods. Soon after four Indians on horseback entered the town, one of whom, Sah-nah-dah-yah, was killed and scalped by Murphy, when Boyd set out for camp.

As Sullivan approached the town about dark on the 13th, he found the enemy, both Indians and rangers drawn up in battle array apparently intending to dispute the further advance of the army; but as the advancing columns assumed their positions in line of battle, and the flanking divisions moved to the right and left, threatening their lines of retreat, a few shots from the howitzers caused them to abandon their position, and retreat across the Canaseraga. The army were engaged until noon of the 14th in destroying the cornfields which were very extensive in the vicinity of the town.

Tuesday, 14th Sept.—At one o'clock left the town crossed the Chenesee flats and forded the river which was about four feet deep and about thirty yards wide and arrived at the capital town of the Chinisees, called the Chinisee Castle.[76] We entered the town about 6 o'clock, found Lieutenant Boyd and one soldier[77] whom they had murdered in an inhuman manner. Said Boyd was one of the party that was sent to reconnoitre a town as is mentioned before. The Chinisee Castle consisted of about one hundred commodius dwelling houses compactly built and pleasantly situated.

Wednesday, 15th Sept.—The whole army[78] (except the guards to which I belonged) were employed in destroying corn from 6 o'clock in the morning till two in the afternoon. In the meantime a white woman[79] with a small child came to us who had been taken prisoner at Weyoming. At about 3 o'clock in the afternoon, we set the town on fire, marched off, recrossed the river and encamped after sunset on the Chinicee Flats.

---

76. Genesee Castle.—This was the great village of the Senecas, the western door of the Long House, located between Cuylerville and the west bank of the Genesee River, in the town of Leicester, Livingston County. It appears on Evans' map as Chenandoanes in 1776, is mentioned as early as 1754 as Chenandanah, and is often called Little Beard's town. Sullivan's official report says: "The Castle consisted of 128 houses mostly large and elegant. The place was beautifully situated, almost encircled with a cleared flat, which extended for a number of miles, where the most extensive fields of corn were waving, and every kind of vegetable that can be conceived."

77. This soldier was named Parker, who with Lieutenant Boyd were made prisoners. They were carried to Little Beard's Town, where Boyd after being tortured in a most cruel manner was beheaded. Parker was beheaded without being tortured. The remains of Boyd and Parker were removed to Mount Hope Cemetery in August, 1842.

78. Several writers claim that Canawaugas, on the west side, and Ohadi and Big Tree on the east side of Genesee River were destroyed in this campaign. No reliable authority has been furnished in support of the theory. Sullivan says distinctly that he went no farther than the great town, beyond which, as he was informed, there was no settlement, and no villages are mentioned in any account as existing on the east side of the river, nor is mention made of any portion of the army being on that side,—on the contrary, several mention the fact, that *all the army* were engaged in the destruction of the town, and cornfields, which, when completed at 2 o'clock on the afternoon of the 15th, *the whole army* came to an about face, and returned on the same route and in same order in which they advanced. Butler left Canawaugas on the morning of the 15th for Niagara.

79. Nathan Davis in his account, before referred to, mentions (continued next page),

Thursday, 16th Sept.—Decamped at 11 o'clock, marched six miles and encamped at the town of Adjutoa at half past five p.m.

Friday 17th.—Decamped at 6 o'clock, marched off and arrived at the town of Haunyuga at one o'clock p.m.

Saturday, 18th Sept.—At 5 o'clock in the morning marched, at 7 o'clock crossed the outlet of a Lake at Cannandagui,[80] and encamped at sunset on the east side of the outlet.

Sunday 19.—At seven o'clock in the morning struck tents, marched at 8 o'clock and arrived at sunset at Canadasago.[81]

Monday, 20th Sept.—At two p.m. struck tents, marched off at 3 o'clock from Canadasago, crossed the outlet of Ceneca Lake and encamped at sunset near the lake.[82] Previous to our march from Canadasago Colonel Butler of the 4th Pennsylvania Regiment was sent with a detachment to the Kiyuga[83] Lake to destroy some Indian settlements that were there. Colonel Gansevort sent with one hundred men to fort Stanwix[84] in order to send down some baggage which was left on the Mohawk River by troops that had been stationed there the preceding year.

Tuesday, 28th.—Struck tents at 8 o'clock, marched at 9, left Can-

---

the incident with additional particulars. Her story was that at the time she and her little boy were taken prisoners, her husband was killed by the savages; that she had lived with the Indians some two years, and when the army entered the town, the day before, the Indians were in such haste to get out it that she could not follow them and finally lost herself in the woods, and thinking it might be Butler's camp she had ventured to show herself. She was taken to the general's quarters and well provided for. During the march the woman and her boy were furnished with a horse. On the third day of the march the child was taken sick and shortly after died. The boy was wrapped in an old blanket and hastily buried. The scene is described as exceedingly touching. She afterward married Roswell Franklin, the first settler of Cayuga County.

80. Present Canandaigua Lake in Ontario County, see note 70.

81. See note 68 for description of this town.

82. This encampment was on Rose Hill in the town of Fayette.

83. Lieutenant Colonel William Butler. See Thomas Grant's account of the march of this detachment.

84. No account has been found of the exact route taken by this detachment. It is supposed they followed the regular Indian trail, the line of which was afterward substantially adopted for the Seneca Turnpike, which passed through Auburn and Onondaga Hill to Fort Stanwix on the Mohawk, on the site of present Rome in Oneida County. On the way the party passed through the Oneida and Tuscarora towns, where every mark of hospitality and friendship was shown the party. They reached Fort Stanwix on the 25th.

daya[85] or Appletown about two miles in the rear, and encamped in the wood, along the east side of the Ceneca Lake, about 4 o'clock in the afternoon.

Wednesday 22nd.—At 6 o'clock the General beat; marched at 8, halted at one o'clock, about one hour for refreshments, and encamped at sunset along the east side Ceneca Lake.

Thursday, 23rd Sept.—Marched at 8 o'clock, left French Catharine about three miles in the rear, and encamped at sunset.[86]

Friday, 24th.—About 6 o'clock in the morning the General beat, marched at 8 o'clock and arrived at the forks of the Tiyuga or Newton. At this place there was a post established by order of General Sullivan, and provision for the army at their return.[87]

Saturday, 25th Sept.—Laid still. An ox and five gallons of rum was given to the officers of each brigade.[88] A *fu-de-joy* was held in consequence of the arrival of the news of Spain declaring us Independent[89] with thirteen rounds of cannon was discharged, followed by two round of musketry interspersed with cannon. The evening was celebrated in our camp with much joy and gladness.[90]

Sunday 26th.—Laid still.

Monday, 27th Sept.—A detachment under the command ———— was sent out and returned at night.[91]

Tuesday 28th.—A detachment under the command of Colonel Cortlandt was sent up the Tiyuga[92] Branch on purpose to destroy some corn. Colonel Butler with his detachment joined us. The inva-

85. Kendaia. See note No. 65 for description of this town.

86. "We lost in this place more than a hundred horses, and it has been called, I suppose, the valley of Horse Heads to this day."—*Nathan Davis' Statement.*

87. During the absence of the army Colonel Reid had constructed a palisaded work at the junction of Newtown Creek and the Chemung just below Sullivan's Mills in Elmira, called in some accounts Fort Reid.

88. There were five brigades.

89 At the same time news was received of "the generous proceedings of Congress in augmenting the subsistence of the officers and men."

90. Thirteen appropriate toasts were drunk. The last was follows: "May the enemies of America be metamorphosed into pack horses and sent on a western expedition against the Indians."—*Lossing's Field Book Rev., 1, 278, note.*

91. "*Sept. 27.*—A large fatigue party was sent up the river nine miles, where they loaded nine boats with corn and other vegetables and brought them down. This evening Mr. Lodge and five men from Colonel Butler came and informed us that the colonel was about ten miles from camp."—*Jenkins' Journal.*

92. Colonel VanCortlandt says he went above Painted Post.

lids were sent to Tiyuga in boats.

Wednesday, 29th Sept.—The General beat at 8 o'clock in the morning, marched at 9 o'clock and encamped in the afternoon three miles below Shemung.

Thursday 30th.—At nine o'clock in the morning marched off and arrived at Tiyuga at 5 o'clock in the afternoon. At our arrival we were saluted with a discharge of thirteen cannon from the Garrison, and an elegant dinner was prepared for the officers.

Friday, Oct. 1, 1779.—Laid still at Tiyuga.[93]

Saturday 2nd.—Laid still. Orders were given to load the boat with stores, artillery, &c., and to demolish the fort[94] the next day.

Sunday, ye 3rd Oct.—Agreeable to the orders of the preceding day the boats were loaded, the fort demolished and everything got in readiness to march the next morning.

Monday, 4th Oct.—At 7 o'clock in the morning the General beat, struck our tents, the army marched at nine from Tiyuga. The boats with the stores, artillery and sick set off at the same time, and encamped at evening at Wysaukin Creek.

Tuesday, the 5th Oct.—The main part of the army embarked on board the boats, the best were mounted on horses, left Wysaukin about 7 o'clock in the morning and arrived at Vanderlips'[95] farm, and stayed at night.

Wednesday ye 6th Oct.—At 6 o'clock in the morning set off and arrived at sunset at Lechawauny[96] about ten miles from Weyoming.

Thursday, 7th Oct.—At 9 o'clock in the morning left Lechawauny and arrived at Weyoming[97] about 1 o'clock in the afternoon.

Friday, Oct. ye 8th.—Laid still.

Saturday, ye 9th.—Remained at Weyoming, but received orders to march at 6 o'clock the next morning.

Sunday, Oct. 10th.—At 6 o'clock next morning were ordered to

---

93. Tioga Point, below present Athens. See note earlier August 11th.
94. Fort Sullivan, built on the narrow isthmus between the two rivers in present village of Athens. See note 57.
95. Van der Lippes. See note 47.
96. Lackawanna. See Note 44. The site of Coxton, ten miles from Wyoming at the upper end of the valley.
97. *Wyoming,* fort and village on the east side of the Susquehanna below present Wilkesbarre. See note earlier 14th June.

march, but on account of our pack horses being strayed we did not march till 2 o'clock in the morning, when we left Weyoming and arrived at Bullock's[98] at dark.

Monday, 11th Oct.—At 9 o'clock in the morning decamped from Bullock's and encamped about two miles through the Shades of Death.[99]

Tuesday, 12th Oct.—At 7 in the morning proceeded on our march. The after part of the day rainy and windy weather, we arrived at White Oak Run[100] at evening and encamped.

Wednesday 13th.—Decamped from White Oak Run at 8 o'clock in the morning and arrived at Brinker's Mills[101] and encamped.

Thursday 14th.—Decamped from Brinker's Mills, marched from thence, and arrived within eleven miles from Easton and encamped[102] on the side of the road in a wood.

Friday, 15th Oct.—Decamped at 7 o'clock, marched for Easton[103] and arrived there about 2 o'clock in the afternoon.

Saturday 16th.—Laid still.

Sunday 17th.—Laid still.

Monday, 18th Oct.—Captain Bevier and myself set out from Easton at 11 o'clock for Marbletown,[104] travelled about twenty miles and put up at the Widow Sweezer's.

---

98. Bullock's, deserted house, seven miles from Wyoming at the Great Meadows, and fifty-eight miles from Easton,—called also Sullivan's camp, from his encamping there June 22. Nathan Bullock resided here at the time of the Wyoming massacre. He had two sons, Amos and Asa, one of whom was a lawyer, both killed in the battle. The father was captured and carried to Canada in 1780.

99. Shades of Death, so called from being a dense forest. Several places in Pennsylvania bore the same name. See note 21.

100. White Oak Run, or Rum Bridge, 33 miles from Easton. See note 26.

101. Brinker's Mills, or Sullivan's Stores, so called "on account of a large house built here, and a quantity of provisions being stored therein for the use of the forces under Major General Sullivan's command."—*Rogers' Journal.* Captain Patterson was in command; nineteen miles from Easton in present town of Hamilton, Monroe County.

102. Encamped near Heller's Tavern at the foot of Blue Mountain, at present Hellerville in town of Plainfield, Northampton County, twelve miles from Easton.

103. "Easton consists of about 150 houses. There are but three elegant buildings in it, and about as many inhabitants that are any ways agreeable. Take them in general they are a very inhospitable set—all High Dutch and Jews."—*Shute's Journal.*

104. Marbletown, a town in Ulster Co., N.Y., west of the Hudson. They appear to have taken the road through Warren and Sussex Counties, N.J.

Tuesday, 19th Oct.—At half past 7 o'clock in the morning, traveled about twenty-seven miles and put up at Cary's Tavern.

Wednesday 20th.—At 7 o'clock a.m., left Cary's, dined at Bard's in Warick,[105] set out from thence and put up at Bruster's Tavern about eleven miles from New Windsor.[106]

Thursday, 21st.—Left Bruster's at 8 o'clock in the morning and arrived at Newburgh, at 2 o'clock in the afternoon.

Friday 22nd.—Set out from Newburgh at 8 o'clock in the morning and arrived at the Poltz[107] and staid that night.

Saturday, 23rd Oct.—At three o'clock in the afternoon set out and arrived home the same night.

From the 23rd Oct., 1779, I remained home till the 9th of Dec., when I set out to join the regiment, which I did on the 15th, and found them employed in building huts for winter quarters, about three miles from Morristown.

(*The Hardenbergh Journal here closes. The Nukerck Journal continues the history of the regiment for the year 1780 and until the five regiments were consolidated near the close of that year.*)

---

105. Warwick on Wawayanda Creek in south west part of Orange County.
106. New Windsor on the Hudson, in Orange County.
107. New Paltz, a post village, on the Wallkill in Ulster County, N.Y.

General Clinton's March Down the Susquehanna

General James Clinton was born in Orange County, New York, August 9th, 1736. He was third son of Colonel Charles Clinton, brother of Governor George Clinton, and father of Governor De-Witt Clinton, of New York. During the French and English war, in 1756, he distinguished himself at the capture of Fort Frontenac, where he was a captain under Bradstreet. Seven years later he commanded the regiments raised to protect the frontiers of Orange and Ulster counties against Indian incursions. In 1775, with the rank of colonel, he accompanied the chivalric Montgomery to Quebec. He was appointed a brigadier, August 9th, 1776, and commanded Fort Clinton when it was attacked in October, 1777, by Sir Henry Clinton; his brother, George Clinton, at same time being in command of Fort Montgomery.

After a gallant defence against superior numbers, the forts were carried by storm, General Clinton being the last man to leave the works. He was stationed at West Point during the greater part of 1778. In 1779 he commanded the brigade of New York troops under General Sullivan. With a force of 1600 men he ascended the Mohawk to Canajoharie, and thence across to Otsego Lake. Here he collected a large number of *batteaux*, and erecting a dam at the foot of the lake, raised the water several feet. By tearing away the dam, an artificial flood was made, on which the *batteaux* floated to the place of meeting at Tioga, the army marching alongside by land. The *Journals* of Lieutenant Van Hovenbergh and Major Beatty give an account of this march.

Major Erkuries Beatty

Major Erkuries Beatty, was born October 9, 1759, son of Rev. Charles Beatty, who came to America from Ireland in 1729. He was an apprentice in Elizabethtown, N.J., at the beginning of the revolution, and served with the Jersey troops; was at Long Island Aug. 9, 1776, under General Sterling, and served as a sergeant at White Plains, Oct 28. He was commissioned an Ensign in the 4th Penn. regiment, with rank from Jan. 3, 1777; was promoted to Lieutenant May 2, and was engaged in the battle of Brandywine, Sept. 11th of same year. He was badly wounded at Germantown, but rejoined his regiment at Valley Forge in January, 1778.

He was at Monmouth June 28 of that year, and shortly after accompanied his regiment to Schoharie, N.Y. He was with Colonel Van Schaick in his expedition against the Onondagas in June, 1779, and with his regiment accompanied General Clinton down the Susquehanna to participate in Sullivan's campaign, during which he wrote a *Journal* covering the period from June 11 to Oct. 22 of that year, of which the following is a part, the original of which is now in the archives of the New York Historical Society, to whose courtesy we are indebted for permission to make a copy. He was at the surrender of Cornwallis Oct. 19, was mustered out of service Nov. 3, 1783, and died at Princeton, N.J., Feb. 23, 1823.

Part of Beatty's Journal, 1779

Monday, Aug. 9.—Agreeable to yesterday's order the General beat at 6 o'clock, the troops marched about 8, excepting three men which was to remain in each boat to take them down the river. The infantry march in front which I now belong to, and the remainder of battalions next, marched on sixteen miles within five miles of Yorkham's[1] where we encamped on a small improvement called Burrows'[2] farm where there was a great many rattlesnakes and very large, there was one killed with fifteen rattles on.

Tuesday 10.—Rained, a little last night and this day till 10 o'clock—marched off the ground at 3 o'clock and went five miles to Yorkham's where we encamped, the men in the boats encamped on the farm which lies on the east side of the river and the remainder on the other side opposite, went on guard tonight.

Wednesday 11.—Marched off this morning at sunrise and proceeded on fourteen miles down the river where we encamped on a small farm, passed several farms today with very poor houses on them and some none, the riflemen in front saw fresh Indian tracks today on the path and found a . . . . . . at one of their . . . . . Today we crossed a large creek called Otego, and passed several Indian encampments, where they had encamped when they were going to destroy Cherry Valley or returning, likewise we passed one of their encampments yesterday, we encamped tonight at Ogden's Farm and very bad encamping ground.

Thursday 12.—Marched off this morning 7 o'clock, had the advanced Guard today, proceeded down the west side of the river as usual, twelve miles came to a small Scotch settlement called Albout[3] on the other side of the river five miles from Unadilla which we

---

1. Joachim Van Valkenberg, afterwards killed in battle near Lake Utsayunthe in 1781.
2. Van Hovenberg's *Journal* says Burris Farms.

burnt, but the people had gone to the enemy this last spring, went on to Unadilla, crossed the river to the east side and encamped, the river was about middle deep when we waded it. This settlement was destroyed by our detachment last fall excepting one house which belonged to one Glasford who went to the enemy this spring, his house was immediately burnt when we came on the ground today. We passed several old Indians encampments where they encamped when they destroyed Cherry Valley, the road middling hilly.

Friday 13th.—This morning very foggy and a great deal of dew. Marched off at 6 o'clock, went two miles, waded the river about three foot deep, proceeded on to Conihunto[4] a small Indian village that was, but was destroyed by our detachment last fall, its fourteen miles from Unadilla.[5] A little below this town there is three or four islands in the river where the Indians raised their corn. On one of those islands our troops encamped with the boats and cattle, the Light Infantry went two miles from Conihunto where they encamped a little after 3 o'clock in the woods. Middle good road today.

Saturday 14th.—Marched this morning at 8 o'clock, very hilly road for the right flank, arrived at the fording two miles from Onoquaga[6] about 2 o'clock which is eight from where we started, the ford being too deep to wade, crossed in our boats to the east side, went over a high hill and got to Onoquaga at 3 o'clock where we encamped on very pretty ground. This town was one of the neatest of the Indian towns on the Susquehanna, it was built on each side of the river with good log houses with stone chimneys and glass windows, it likewise

3. Albout.—A Scotch, Tory settlement on the east side of the Unadilla River, five miles above Unadilla, was burned Aug. 12, 1779, by Clinton's detachment. Most of the Scotch Settlers went to Canada at the beginning of the difficulties; those who remained were more in sympathy with the British than with the Americans.
4. Conihunto, called Gunnagunter by Van Hovenberg, an Indian town fourteen miles below Unadilla, destroyed by Colonel William Butler in 1778. It appears to have been on the west side of the river.
5. Unadilla, an Indian town at the junction of the Unadilla with the Susquehanna, destroyed by Colonel William Butler in 1778. "Returning to Unadilla, that settlement, on both sides of the river was burned, as also a grist-mill and saw-mill, the only ones in the Susquehanna Valley."—*Letter of Colonel William Butler.*
6. Onoquaga, an Indian town on both sides of the Susquehanna River, eight miles below Conihunto near present Ouaquaga in the town of Colesville, Broome Co. When destroyed by Colonel Butler in 1778 he mentions a lower or Tuscarora town three miles below, this would be near present Windsor. The old fort mentioned is probably one built for the Indians by Sir William Johnson in 1756. Rev. Gideon Hawley was a missionary here at an early date.

had a church and burying ground and a great number of apple-trees, and we likewise saw the ruins of an old fort which formerly was here many years ago. The Indians abandoned this town last fall when they heard of our detachment coming to destroy it, they had but just left it when we came in it, but we did not catch any of them, but burnt their town to ashes, and the detachment returned. This evening we fired an evening gun.

Sunday 15th.—Very heavy dew this morning, went on guard, the army remain at Onoquago today quiet, no news stirring as I hear of particular.

Monday 16th.—This morning a very heavy dew and fog, which is very customary in this country, was relieved of my guard and the day proved exceedingly warm, a heavy shower of rain this afternoon, at 12 o'clock Major Church with the 4th P. Regiment went out five or six miles to meet 400 or 500 Militia[7] who we expected to join us here, but he returned in the evening and saw nothing of them.

Tuesday 17th.—Marched off from Onoquaga this morning 8 o'clock, proceeded down the river three miles to one of the Tuscarora towns, which was burnt by one of our Detachments last fall, here waded the river about four feet deep to the west side, went on one mile when we came to another of the Tuscarora towns called Shawhiangto[8] consisting of ten or twelve houses which we burnt, then marched on over a very barren mountainous country ten or twelve miles, came to a Tuscarora settlement called Ingaren[9] consisting of five or six houses, but a good deal scattered, encamped at the lower end of the settlement after burning the houses, here they had planted a good deal of corn, potatoes, &c., which we destroyed, a few yards in front of our company's encamping ground there was a tanfat farm with several hides at a tannery which the soldiers got, and close by it they discovered in a little hole, a man which was laid there and a little

---

7. Colonel Pawling, commanding a regiment of New York levies, was to meet Clinton at this point, but arriving after the army had passed, they returned to Wawarsing.
8. Shawhiangto, a small Tuscarora town four miles below Onoquago, burned by General Clinton August 17, 1779; it contained ten or twelve houses, located on the west side of the river, near present Windsor in Broome County.
9. Ingaren, a small Tuscarora town, at or near Great Bend in Susquehanna County, Penn. It was called Tuscarora by Van Hovenberg, and described as being sixteen miles from the camp, four miles below Chenango River; and twelve miles by land and twenty by water, from Onoquaga, where the army encamped on the 16th. Was destroyed by General Clinton, August 17, 1779.

dirt thrown over him just to cover him. We had his head uncovered, but he was too putrified, we could not discover whether he was a white man or Indian but supposed to be a white man, as there was a Scotch Bonnet found near him. Marched today fifteen miles.

Wednesday 18th.—Marched off from Ingaren 7 o'clock through a very fine rich country very well timbered but poorly watered, scarce any; arrived at Chinango River at 4 o'clock where we forded it about four feet deep, and almost as wide as the Susquehanna but not so deep, as soon as we got over we halted and Major Parr with 100 men went up the river to destroy the Chinango town[10] which lay four miles up the river, but when we came there, we found the town was burnt, which consisted of about twenty houses. It seems when the Indians evacuated it last winter they destroyed it, therefore we returned and found the army encamped two mile below the Chinango River. Marched today twenty-two miles, and burnt several Indian houses on the road.

This evening came up the river two runners who informed us that General Poor with 1000 men was within nine miles of us coming to meet us and that Genl. Sullivan lay at the mouth of the Tyoga and that he had sent part of his army up to Shamong which they had destroyed, and had returned to General Sullivan with the loss of nine men killed and some more wounded, which was in small skirmishing. The Indians had taken off all their [property] from Shamong, except a few cattle which our people got.

Thursday 19th.—Marched this morning 7 o'clock, went two miles where we burnt seven or eight houses on the east side of the river, four miles further at the Chuggnuts[11] we fell in with General Poor's army who was ready to march, they had burnt this settlement which lies on the east side of the river about twenty houses, made no halt

---

10. Chenango, also called Otsiningo, an important Indian town located four miles north of Binghamton on the Chenango river, in present town of Chenango, near the present village of the same name. The twenty-two miles travel mentioned, evidently includes the march up the Chenango to this town, and from thence to the camp. Van Hovenberg estimates the day's march of the army at sixteen miles. Many writers incorrectly locate this town at Binghamton.

11. Choconut, or *Chugnutt*, an important Indian town of fifty or sixty houses, mostly on the south side of the Susquehanna at the mouth of Big Choconut Creek, on the site of the present village of Vestal, in town of Vestal, Broome county. Burned Aug. 19, 1779, by General Poor's detachment which encamped on the north side of the river near present Union where the two detachments united. General Clinton's camp the same night, was six miles distant up the river.

here but went on four mile, General Clinton's army in front and General Poor's in the rear. Came to a middling large creek where we made a halt for one hour, then marched on twelve miles without halting and arrived at Owego[12] about sundown after a very fatiguing march of twenty-two miles. This afternoon fell a small shower of rain.

Friday 20th.—Rained a little last night, and successively all this day therefore did not move, went a party down to Owego town which lies one mile lower down and burnt it, consisted of about twenty houses.

Saturday 21.—Clear weather this morning but a very heavy fog, marched a little after 7 o'clock, forded Owego Creek which is about —— one third of the Susquehanna, at this place it was about three feet deep and about fifty yards wide—Went through the —— of Owego town, crossed a pretty large brook, went twelve miles, halted at a small brook one hour for refreshment. Proceed on three miles further when we encamped at 4 o'clock opposite Fitzgerald's Farm, (see note following), in the woods, it is a very fine farm but no house on it, nor any body living on it. On this ground where we encamped Mr. Sawyers a man who was made prisoner by Indians, along with his neighbour Mr. Cowley who both lived on the head of the Delaware, after the Indians having them so far on their Journey, they rose in the night killed the Indians which was three or four and made their escape, we saw the —— of the Indians —— when we came on the ground. Today we met with a bad accident, two of our boats of ammunition overset in the river and damaged a good many boxes of cartridges and a few casks of powder, tonight went on guard.

> Note.—Manckatawangum, or Red Bank, here called Fitzgerald's Farm, appears to have been on the south side of the Susquehanna, in the town of Nichols, nearly opposite the village of Barton. Major Norris' *Journal*, in going up, says on the 16th the detachment "encamped near the ruins of an old town called Macktowanuck" (see note following August 14th, Journal of the Campaign); Lieutenant Jenkins' *Journal*; says "ten miles from Tioga at a place called Manckatawangum or *Red Bank*," and mentions encamping at same point on the return march. A table of distances in Canfield's Journal says "from the mouth of

---

12. Owagea, an Indian town of about twenty houses. Occupied in 1779, located on Owego Creek about a mile from the Susquehanna near the present village of Owego in Tioga County. General Poor's detachment encamped Aug. 17th on the site of present village, where was a small Indian Hamlet. Owagea was burned Aug. 19.

the Tioga (Chemung) to Mackatowando ten miles." This would locate the Indian town at or near present Barton. On the Tioga county map, Mohontowonga Farm appears on the south side of the river opposite Barton, and an island in the river named Mohontowango.

Early in the spring of 1779, two men named Sawyer and Cowley were captured near Harpersfield, by four Schoharie Indians, named Han Yerry, Seth's Henry, Adam and Nicholas. One of the captives was an Irishman, the other a Scotchman. They were refugees from Harpersfield, who had sought safety in Schoharie at the beginning of the difficulties. The prisoners could not speak Dutch, which the Indians understood, nor could the Indians understand English. When captured, they claimed by signs to be friends of the King, and were not only willing, but anxious to accompany their captors.

The prisoners set off with such apparent willingness on the journey, that the Indians did not think it necessary to bind them, but permitted them to procure wood and water. They had been captives eleven days without finding a favourable opportunity for escape, but on arriving at a deserted hut at this point, the captives were sent to cut wood a few rods distant, using for this purpose an axe belonging to one of the prisoners. On such occasions, usually one cut and the other carried to the camp fire; but this time, while Cowley was chopping, and Sawyer waiting for an armful, the latter took from his pocket a newspaper, and pretended to read its contents to his fellow, but really proposed a plan for regaining their liberty.

After procuring a sufficient quantity of wood, and partaking of a scanty supper, they laid down for the night as usual, a prisoner between two Indians. When the Indians were sound asleep, the prisoners arose, secured the guns, shaking the priming from them, Sawyer securing the tomahawk of Han Yerry, and Cowley the axe. At a given signal, the blows descended, and the weapons sank deep into the brain of their victims, but unfortunately, Sawyer in attempting to free his weapon from the skull, drew the handle from its socket.

These two Indians were killed, but the noise awoke the others, who instantly sprung to their feet; as Seth's Henry arose, he received a blow partially warded off by his right arm, but his shoulder was laid open and he fell back stunned; the fourth,

71

as he was about to escape, received a heavy blow in the back from the axe; he fled to a swamp nearby and died. On returning to the hut and consulting as to what course they should pursue, Seth's Henry, who had recovered, but feigned death, again sprang to his feet, caught his rifle and snapped it at one of the prisoners, ran out of the hut and disappeared.

The two friends primed the remaining guns and kept vigilant watch until daylight to guard against surprise. They set out in the morning to return, but did not dare to pursue the route they came, very properly supposing there were more of the enemy in the vicinity, to whom the surviving Indian would communicate the fate of his comrades. They re-crossed the river in a bark canoe which they had used the preceding afternoon, and then directed their course for the frontier settlements. On the first night, Cowley, carried away by the excitement was deranged for hours, and his companion was fearful that his raving would betray them, but reason returned with daylight.

As they had feared, a party of Indians was soon in hot pursuit—from a hill they saw ten or a dozen in the valley below; but they concealed themselves beneath a sheltering rock, and remained there one night and two days. When there an Indian dog came up to them, but after smelling for some time, went away without barking. On the third night they saw the enemy's fires literally all around them. They suffered much from exposure to the weather, and still more from hunger, but finally arrived at a frontier settlement in Pennsylvania, and afterward returned to Schoharie, where they were welcomed as though risen from the dead. Sawyer is said to have died many years after in Williamstown, Mass., and Cowley in Albany.—*Symm's Schoharie*, 291, 2, 3.

Sunday 22nd.—Marched off this morning 7 o'clock, proceeded on, we crossed two middling large brooks. Arrived at Tyoga 11 o'clock, where we found Genl. Hand's brigade encamped one mile above the mouth of the Tyoga where they was building four block houses, the other troops was encamped over the point which was Generals Poor's and Maxwell's brigades, we encamped on the right of the whole. On our coming into camp we was saluted by thirteen pieces of cannon which was returned by our two little pieces on the river. We found General Hand's brigade under arms with a band of music which

played beautiful as we passed by them, We encamped on a very . . . .
. . pretty piece of ground and spent the remainder of the day in seeing our friends in the different regiments, likewise when we arrived
here our infantry was disbanded and ordered to join their respective
regiments. Very heavy shower of rain this afternoon. Marched seven
miles today.

Expedition Against the Cayugas

MARCH OF COLONEL BUTLER ALONG THE EAST SIDE OF CAYUGA LAKE

On the return march, when the army reached Kanadaseaga on September 20, Lieutenant Colonel Butler commanding the Fourth Pennsylvania regiment was detached with six hundred men, with orders to proceed around the north end of Cayuga lake, and devastate the country of the Cayugas on the east side of the lake. At the same time a force under Lieutenant Colonel Henry Dearborn was ordered to move along the west side, the two detachments to unite at the head of the lake and from thence to join the main army at Catharinestown.

William Butler was the second of five brothers, all of whom served with distinction in the Revolution and the succeeding wars. Their names were Richard, William, Thomas, Percival and Edward. Thomas, the third brother, is said to have been born in Pennsylvania in 1754, and Richard the elder in Ireland, so that William was either born in America, or came here from Ireland when very young. He was commissioned Lieutenant Colonel October 25, 1776, on the organization of the Fourth Pennsylvania Regiment. Immediately after the battle of Monmouth, in which he bore an important part, his regiment and six companies of Morgan's riflemen were sent to Schoharie County, New York, where he was actively engaged in protecting the frontier settlements from the marauding parties of Tories and Indians.

After the Wyoming massacre in 1778, as a part of the aggressive policy determined on by Washington, he marched to the Delaware, and descended that stream for two days, and from thence moved across the country to the Susquehanna at Unadilla in pursuit of the enemy, who fled at his approach. From here he moved down to Onoquaga, which was a well built town, with many good farm houses in the vicinity belonging to the Tories, located on both sides of the river. He destroyed Onoquaga, and a Tuscarora town lower down, Conihunto eight miles above, and Unadilla, with the grist and saw mill there, the only ones in the valley, and forced the enemy to remove westward to the Chemung where they were found by Sullivan the next year. He was in garrison in the Middle Fort of Schoharie during the winter, and in August, 1779, accompanied Clinton down the Susquehanna to Tioga point where he was transferred to General Hand's Brigade August 23rd of that year.

This was the Colonel Butler to whom General Sullivan entrusted the responsible duties of conducting this important expedition, second only in importance to that of the main army. Two journals give an account of Colonel Butler's march, *viz.*, Thomas Grant, who appears to have been one of the surveying party under Captain Lodge, and George Grant, Sergeant Major of the Third New Jersey regiment, the latter evidently copied from some other journal.

Part of Thomas Grant's Journal

Sept. 20.—This day a detachment of six hundred men with a sufficiency of officers under the command of Colonel Wm. Butler were sent into the Cayuga country, with which detachment I was ordered. They marched from Cannadesago at 3 o'clock p.m. Marched this day eight miles to an Indian town by the name of Scawyace[1] where about eight acres of corn was destroyed.

Sept 21.—The detachment marched this morning at 7 o'clock a.m. sixteen and a half miles to a small Indian settlement[2] one and a half miles short of Cayuga Castle, where we encamped for the night. At eight and a half miles crossed the outlet of Cayuga, which in breadth was about seventy perches, and more than middle deep to the men. Near the outlet we destroyed two Indian houses. The name of the place Choharo[3] and destroyed on the lake in different places ——

1. Scawyace or *Long Falls*, an important Indian town of eighteen houses, located on the north bank of Seneca River at present site of Waterloo, in Seneca County. It was partially destroyed on August 8, during the advance of the army by a party of volunteers under Colonel Harper. George Grant mentions the fact of "several fish ponds abounding opposite the town." These were circular enclosures of stone from thirty to forty feet in diameter, built up on the rocky bed of the stream, where the water was neither very deep or rapid, so constructed as to permit the water to pass through, but to retain the fish.
2. Gewauga, a small hamlet on the present site of Union Springs in the town of Springport, on the east side of Cayuga Lake.
3. Choharo.—This was the Tichero or St. Stephen of the Jesuit Relations, said to signify *the place of rushes*, located at the foot of Cayuga Lake on the east side, at the exact point where the bridge of the Middle Turnpike left the east shore. The trail across the marsh followed the north bank of an ancient channel of the Seneca River, which at an early day took that course. The turnpike afterward followed substantially the line of the trail and crossed the present line of the Cayuga and Seneca Canal three times between Mud Lock and the old Demont tavern on the opposite side of the marsh. The salt springs mentioned by Father Raffeix (continued next page),

houses and —— acres of corn, but saw no enemy. The general course since we crossed the outlet, nearly south, the road not more than half a mile from the lake at furthest, the land middling.

Sept. 22, 1779.—Marched this day at 6 o'clock a.m. two miles to the Cayuga Castle,[4] an Indian town of that name containing in number about 15 very large square log houses. I think the building superior to any yet have seen. [Here] cattle were killed and three days beef issued to the troops. The fatigue parties were sent to destroy the corn to the amount of about 110 acres, though not all destroyed this day. Two other towns were discovered, one twenty-three and a half miles from the Seneca Lake, which we called Upper Cayuga,[5] containing fourteen large houses, the other about two miles east of the castle which we called Cayuga,[6] containing thirteen houses. The troops were all employed this day in destroying corn till after dark. We found at this town apples, peaches, potatoes, turnips, onions, pumpkins, squashes, and vegetables of various kinds and great plenty.

Sept. 23, 1779.—This day the troops were employed till 3 o'clock p.m. in finishing the destruction of the corn and burning the aforementioned towns within. Marched five miles to an Indian town by the name of Chandot[7] or Peach Town, remarkable for a large peach orchard containing —— hundred fine thriving peach trees, likewise —— acres of corn. This town contained about twelve or fourteen houses chiefly old buildings. Part of the corn was destroyed this evening.

Sept. 24, 1779.—This morning the troops were employed in finishing the destruction of the corn and peach trees. At 10 o'clock a.m.

---

in 1672, were on the west side of the marsh about half a mile north of the N.Y.C. Rail Road bridge, and on the bank of the ancient river channel.

4. Cayuga Castle, an Indian town containing fifteen very large houses of squared logs, located on the south line of the town of Springport in Cayuga County, on the north bank of Great Gully brook, and from one to two miles from the lake.

5. Upper Cayuga, an Indian town of fourteen very large houses located near the north line of the town of Ledyard in Cayuga County, on the south bank of Great Gully brook, and as appears on the map, between one and two miles from the lake.

6. East Cayuga, or *Old Town*, contained thirteen houses located in the south-east corner of the town of Springport, as indicated on the map, from three to four miles from the lake. A site in the south-west corner of Fleming was a site of this town at about this date.

7. Chonodote, so named on Captain Lodge's map, an Indian town of fourteen houses, on the site of present Aurora in Cayuga County; according to George Grant's journal it contained fifteen hundred peach trees.

fire was set to this town and the detachment went off the ground. Marched this day sixteen and a half miles and encamped on a pleasant hill[8] near a fine creek about one hour after dark. The land we passed this day well timbered, and the soil very good, but very scarce of water. Nine miles from Chondote we crossed a stream of water which fell over rocks eighty feet perpendicular. Three miles from [this] we crossed a second stream[9] which fell about fifty feet perpendicular, which empty themselves into Cayuga Lake. Saw no enemy this day. The general course S. 30° E.

Sept. 25, 1779.—Marched this morning about 6 o'clock and encamped at an Indian town three and a half miles above Cayuga Lake. The town appeared to be just consumed, supposed to be burnt by a detachment from General Sullivan's army.[10] The town was situated on a rising ground in a large, beautiful valley. The soil equal to or rather superior to any in the country, through which runs several fine streams of water, the first a creek about four poles wide, which falls from the mountain on the east side of the valley about 120 feet perpendicular into which creek three other fine streams empty, the second creek is the principal supply of the Cayuga Lake navigable for large canoes or boats to the town.

[*The journal here ends abruptly*]

---

8. On the hill north of Ludlowville.
9. The first of these falls was probably on Mill Creek, two and a half miles southwest of Northville; the second near Lake Ridge in the town of Lansing.
10. Coreorgonel was burned by the detachment under Colonel Dearborn. See his account September 24, and note 7.

Part of George Grant's Journal

Sept. 20, 1779.—I return to the 20th to follow Colonel Butler, who left us at Kanadasago, and proceeded along the outlet of Seneca Lake for eight miles and halted at Schoyerre, formerly destroyed by Colonel Harper.

Sept. 21.—Early this morning a party of 200 men under the command of Major Scott was despatched to destroy corn, &c., the remainder with Colonel Butler, proceeded on forward. Seven miles of the road was very bad, the land poor and barren, and no water. They then entered on an excellent swamp which produces fine timber, the soil exceeding rich and fertile. This extends for four miles, when they reached Caiuga Lake. This they crossed at a place wading it to their breasts in water, where they halted waiting for Major Scott and his party. As soon as they had joined, they proceeded along the side of the lake side, the land excellent, the timber large and the country level and well watered. Came to a habitation within one mile of Caiuga town and encamped eighteen miles from Scoyerre.

Sept. 22.—Marched to Caiuga[1] one mile distant. This town is large and commodius, consisting of 50 houses mostly well built. The party went immediately to destroying corn, &c., with which this place

---

1. Goi-o-gouen, of the Jesuit Relations, and site of the Mission of St. Joseph, called also Cayuga Castle, and the same described as three towns by Thomas Grant under the names of Cayuga Castle, fifteen houses; upper Cayuga, containing fourteen houses; and Cayuga, containing thirteen houses. The houses were very much scattered, and on both sides of Great Gully brook on the south line of the town of Springport in Cayuga County. Greenhalgh, an English trader, passed through the Cayuga country in 1677, and found them there occupying "three towns about a mile distant from each other; they are not stockaded. They do consist in all of about one hundred houses and intend next spring to build all their houses together and stockade them. They have abundance of corn, and lie within two or three miles of Lake Tichero."

abounds, but the water very bad and scarce. Here was found some salt of the Indians making from the Salt Springs[2] which are in this country. Found several muskets here, branded with the brand of the United States; also a few regimental coats, blue, faced with white.

Sept. 23.—The most part of the day taken up in destroying scattering towns, corn, &c., within two or three miles all around this town. About 4 o'clock marched for another town[3] distant four miles but could not learn any name for it, and here halted for the night.

Sept. 24.—This morning went to destroying corn, beans, and orchards. Destroyed about 1500 peach trees, besides apple trees and other fruit trees. This town consisted of thirteen houses. Then marched for eighteen miles, the first twelve the land exceeding good, the other six not extraordinary.

Sept. 25.—Marched for ten and a half miles the road mostly bad, having to ascend and descend extreme steep and difficult mountains, then through thick and difficult swamps. Passed the end of Caiuga Lake and halted at De-ho-riss-kana-dia[4] which they found burnt and the corn partly destroyed. Here was found the Rev. Dr. Kirkland's horse, supposed to be left here by the party who destroyed the corn, &c.

Sept. 26.—Marched for eight and a half miles through the Great Swamp.

Sept. 27.—Marched for seventeen miles, fifteen of which was through the above swamp. Most part of the way, they had to steer by the sun, there not being the least semblance of a road or path. A man of this party died suddenly.

Sept. 28.—Marched for one mile and crossed the outlet (inlet) of Caiuga Lake, and came upon ground occupied by the army on the night of the 31st of August, from there to Kanawaholee,[5] where they joined the main body of Sullivan's army.

---

2. These salt springs were located on the opposite side of the river from Choharo, see note 3, Thomas Grant's *Journal*. Luke Swetland, a prisoner in 1778, made salt at these springs, which he says was of excellent quality.

3. Chonodote. See note 7, Thomas Grant's journal.

4. Coreorgonel, two miles south of Ithaca, destroyed by the detachment under Colonel Dearborn on the 24th. See note 7 Colonel Dearborn's journal.

5. Kanawlohalla, on the site of present Elmira. See Journal of Campaign, note following 31st August.

March of Colonel Dearborn Along the West Side of Cayuga Lake

On the return march, after crossing the outlet of Seneca Lake east of Kanadaseaga, the army encamped on the high ground at Rose Hill, near the east shore of the lake. Here Lieutenant Colonel Henry Dearborn commanding the Third New Hampshire regiment, was detached with two hundred men and ordered to march along the west shore of Cayuga lake to co-operate with Colonel Butler in devastating the country of the Cayugas.

Colonel Dearborn was born in Hampton, N.H., in March, 1751. He was a captain at Bunker Hill, and accompanied Arnold in the march through the woods against Quebec, in which expedition he was captured. He was exchanged in 1777, and soon after was appointed Major of Scammel's regiment. At Saratoga he commanded a separate battalion under General Gates, and was afterwards at Monmouth, where he distinguished himself and the regiment by a gallant charge. In 1779 Colonel Scammel was acting as Adjutant General of the army, leaving Lieutenant Colonel Dearborn in command of the regiment during Sullivan's campaign. He was at the siege of Yorktown in 1781, and afterward on garrison duty at Saratoga and West Point until 1784. He served two terms in Congress, was for eight years secretary of war under Jefferson, and in the war of 1812 was senior Major General of the army.

In 1822 he was minister to Portugal, from whence he returned after two years' service, and died in Roxbury, Mass., June 6, 1829. After his death, his son, Henry Alexander Scammel Dearborn, collected and arranged the valuable papers of his father, transcribed the journals, which extended through the entire period of the revolution, and added important historical sketches, the whole making forty-five large volumes handsomely bound in morocco, the exterior approximating in elegance to the inestimable value of the material within. On the death of the son, all of these, excepting seven volumes, were taken apart, and the contents, made up of valuable autograph letters of the revolutionary period, scattered to the four winds by a sale at public auction.

The original manuscript *Journal* of Sullivan's campaign fell into the hands of Dr. John H.S. Fogg, of Boston. The manuscript *Orderly Book of Valley Forge*, was purchased by John H. Osborne, Esq., of Auburn. The seven volumes, containing no autographs, were reserved at the sale and remain intact In one of these is the *Journal* kept during Sullivan's campaign, as transcribed by the son, of which the following is an extract:

Part of Colonel Dearborn's Journal, 1779

Sept. 21.—I was ordered with 200 men to proceed to the west side of the Cayuga Lake, from thence down the side of the lake to the south end, to burn and destroy such houses and corn as might be found and to intercept the Cayugas if they attempted to escape Colonel Butler. At 8 o'clock I marched, proceeded an east course about eight miles and found three *wigwams* in the woods[1] with some small patches of corn, squashes, water-melons and cucumbers and fifteen horses which we could not take. Destroyed this village, proceeded four miles to the lake where we found a very pretty town of ten houses[2] and a considerable quantity of corn, all which we burnt.

We discovered another small town about a mile above this, we likewise destroyed. This place is called Skannautenate.[3] After destroying this town I marched on one mile, and came to a new town[4] consisting of nine houses which we destroyed, and proceeded one mile and

1. This hamlet appears to have been located on the farm of Thomas Shankwiller, near the south-east corner of lot 15 in the town of Fayette, Seneca County, probably on Sucker Brook.
2. A town of ten houses, located on the west bank of Cayuga Lake at the northeast corner of the town of Fayette, in Seneca County, about a mile and a half from present Canoga village. Destroyed Sept. 21, 1779.
3. Skannayutenate, a small village located about forty rods from the shore of the lake, on the south bank of Canoga Creek, about half a mile north-east of present Canoga village. On the north bank of the creek, between the site of the old Indian town and the north and south road passing through Canoga, is said to be the birthplace of the renowned Seneca orator, Sagoyewatha or Red Jacket. Destroyed Sept. 21, 1779.
4. Newtown—An Indian village of nine houses, located on the west bank of Cayuga Lake, on the Disinger Farm, a mile south of present Canoga village, and directly opposite the village of Union Springs on the east side of the lake. Destroyed Sept. 21, 1779.

found one large house which we set fire to, and marched two miles and encamped. The land we marched over this day is exceeding fine.

Sept. 22.—I marched half an hour before sunrise, proceeded five miles and came to the ruins of a town which a part of our army burnt when it was advancing who missed their way and happened to fall in with it, half a mile distant found a large field of corn and three houses. We gathered the corn and burnt it in the houses. This town is called Swahyawana.[5] Moved on five miles and came to a wigwam with three squaws and one young Indian who was a cripple. I took two of the squaws who were about forty years of age and marched on three miles and found one hut and a field of corn which was burnt. Went four miles further and encamped.

Sept. 23.—Marched at sunrise, proceeded without any path or track, or any person who was ever in this part of the country before to guide us, and the land so horribly rough and brushy that it was difficult to advance, however with great labour and difficulty we proceeded eight miles to the end of a long cape[6] which I expected was the end of the lake. We then marched off two or three miles from the lake, and went by a point of compass eight miles to the end of the lake and encamped. This lake is forty miles in length and from two to five miles in width, and runs nearly No. and So. parallel to the Seneca Lake which is from eight to ten miles distant.

Sept. 24.—Marched at sunrise, proceeded three miles on the high land and came to an old path which led us to two huts and some cornfields, which we burnt. I then sent several parties in different directions to look for a large town that I had been informed was not many miles from the end of the lake. The parties found ten or twelve scattering houses and a number of large cornfields on and near the stream that falls into the lake. After burning several fields of corn and

5. Swahyawana, was on the farm of Edward R. Dean, in the north-east corner of the town of Romulus, in Seneca County, on the north bank of Sinclair Hollow Creek, near the shore of the lake, and almost exactly opposite the important town of Chonodote, on the east side, at site of present Aurora. Was burned September 6, by a party that wandered from the track of the main army when they passed up on the east side of the lake.

6. Taghanic Point, formerly known as Goodwin's Point. The bank of the lake both north and south of this, is very much cut up with ravines, and the lake shore is too rocky and precipitous for an Indian path. For several miles the trail was back two miles from the lake, along the heads of the ravines, probably passing through Hayt's corners and Ovid Centre. From this high ground the lake appears to end at Taghanic Point.

houses they discovered the town, three miles from the lake, on the above mentioned stream, which contained twenty-five houses and is called Coreorgonel, (see note following), and is the capital of a small nation or tribe. My party was employed from 9 till sunset in destroying the town and corn. I expected to have met Colonel Butler with his party at this town.

Note. Coreorgonel, called De-ho-riss-kanadia by George Grant, was located on the west side of Cayuga inlet, about three miles from the end of the lake, and two miles south of Ithaca. The main village was on a high ground south of the school-house on the farm of James Fleming, nearly opposite Buttermilk Falls. Several skeletons have been exhumed here within a few years, and the usual variety of relics found, such as hatchets, *wampum*, beads, &c. A solitary apple-tree still remains, a fit memento to represent the race by which it was planted. When first known to the whites there were five boles starting from the ground, but these are now reduced to two, and are probably shoots from the original tree cut down or girdled by Dearborn. The town was destroyed September 24, 1779.

At this time it contained twenty-five houses, besides ten or twelve scattered between the main village and the lake. Colonel Butler after passing up on the east side of Cayuga Lake halted here on the 25th, and found Rev. Dr. Kirkland's horse in the vicinity of the smoking ruins.

A peculiar interest is attached to this locality and village, from the fact that here the representatives of a once powerful people, sought to preserve for a brief period, the last remaining spark of a council fire that from time immemorial had burned brilliantly in the presence of assembled nations, numbering their warriors by thousands. They were called by the Iroquois Toderichroones, one of the tribes known to the English as Catawbas, sometimes called Saponies. They formerly resided between the Potomac and Roanoke Rivers, east of the Alleghanies.

A most inveterate hostile feeling existed between them and the Iroquois, which reached back to near the middle of the seventeenth century. A peace was arranged as early as 1685, through negotiations with the government of Virginia, and again what was expected to be a "lasting peace" and firm alliance, was concluded in 1714, but in the night after the close of the council, the Iroquois deputies, while reposing in fancied security were treacherously murdered while asleep.

This aroused the Iroquois to vengeance, and the war was renewed with unexampled ferocity, with a determination to totally extirpate the base, faithless and treacherous people. In 1717 through the intercession of Governor Hunter, at the request of Governor Spottswood of Virginia, a truce was arranged, and in 1722 delegates from the Five Nations met Governor Spottswood at Albany to conclude what was to be an "everlasting peace," in which the Iroquois bound themselves not to cross the Potomac or go over the Alleghanies, without a passport from the Governor of New York, Governor Spottswood engaging that the tribes in his locality should not pass to the north or west of same lines.

The tribes mentioned by the Governor were the "Nottoways, Meherins, Nansemonds, Pamunkeys, Chicohominys, and the Christanna Indians whom you call Toderichroones," and others—in all, ten nations. This council was conducted with great formality, and valuable presents were presented, among which were a "*fine coronet*" and a "*gold horse shoe*" with an inscription. In 1738 they were again at war, and in 1742 at peace. In 1731 Governor Clinton says "the Governor of South Carolina sent six chiefs of the Catawbas, to make peace with the Five Nations," and says that "they had been at war as long as anyone in this country can remember."

In 1753 Sir William Johnson mentions the fact that the Cayugas "*are about to strengthen their castle by taking in the*Tedarighroones." In the same year they are mentioned as attending a conference at Mt. Johnson and are described as "one of the nine confederate nations." The town is indicated at the head of Cayuga Lake on the Guy Johnson map of 1771, in the same position where it was found by Colonel Dearborn in 1779, under the name of Todevighrono, the name of the people. In 1750 Zeisberger, the Moravian missionary, passed through this valley while on his way to visit the Cayugas, but makes no mention of an Indian village in the vicinity.

Undoubtedly they settled there in the summer of 1753. Their cleared fields were found on the present site of Ithaca on the first settlement of the country by the whites and were the first lands occupied in the county. The town is indicated but not

86

named on the map of Mr. Lodge, the surveyor who accompanied Colonel Butler's detachment. To stand on the identical spot from which this people sunk into oblivion, appeared like standing on the grave of a nation.

Their history, the beginning of which extends far back into the unknown and unattainable, ends where that of civilization begins, and adds another name to the long list of extinguished nationalities that preceded us in sovereignty. Here their council fire, fanned by the last expiring breath of a once brave and numerous people, was extinguished forever.

Sept. 25.—Marched at sunrise for Catherine's Town, where I was ordered to join the main army. Proceeded a due west course over a very rough, mountainous country eighteen miles, and at 4 o'clock reached the town, but the army was gone forward. Advanced six miles in what is called the Bear Swamp and encamped.

Sept. 26.—Marched at sunrise and at 12 o'clock joined the main army at Kanawalahola which is four miles from where we fought the enemy on the 29th of August. The army had a day of rejoicing here in consequence from the news of Spain.

Sept. 27.—Some detachments were sent up the Teago River to destroy such houses and corn fields as they might find.

Sept. 28.—The same parties that were sent out yesterday were sent again further up the river to destroy a Tory settlement which was discovered yesterday, and a large detachment was sent off to complete the destruction of the corn, &c., at and about New Town. At 12 o'clock Colonel Butler and his party arrived in camp. In their route round the lake they destroyed several towns and a vast quantity of corn.

Recapitulation

INDIAN TOWNS DESTROYED IN SULLIVAN'S CAMPAIGN, 1779.

1. Newtychanning, an Indian town of about twenty houses, located on the west side of the Susquehanna, near North Towanda, Bradford County, Pa. Destroyed by Colonel Proctor, Aug. 8, 1779.

2. Old Chemung, an Indian town partially abandoned, located on the north bank of Chemung River, half a mile above present Chemung village. Destroyed Aug. 13, 1779

3. New Chemung, an Indian town of fifty or sixty houses, located on the left bank of the Chemung River, three miles above the present village of Chemung, in Chemung County. Destroyed Aug. 13, 1779. See note 59.

4. Newtown, an Indian town of about twenty houses, located on the north bank of Chemung River, five miles below Elmira. It gave the name to the battle fought near it Aug. 29, 1779. Destroyed August 31, 1779.

5. A village of twenty to thirty new houses, located on both sides of Baldwin's Creek, about a mile and a half from Chemung River, at the exact point where General Poor commenced the ascent of the hill. Destroyed Aug. 29, 1779.

6. A small village on Baldwin's Creek, near the works of the enemy, at Newtown, the timbers of which were used in the construction of the fortifications.

7. A small village on Seely Creek, near present Southport, south of Elmira. Destroyed Aug. 30, 1779.

8. Albout, a Scotch, Tory settlement on the east side the Unadilla, about five miles above Unadilla. Burned August 12, 1779, by General Clinton.

9. Shawhiangto, a small Tuscarora town, four miles below Ono-quago, of ten or twelve houses, located on the west side of the Susquehanna, near present Windsor, in Broome County. Burned August 17, 1779, by General Clinton.

10. Ingaren, a Tuscarora town of five or six houses, sometimes called Tuscarora, at Great Bend, Susquehanna County, Penn. Destroyed Aug. 17, 1779, by General Clinton.

11. Otsiningo or *Chenango*, an important Indian town abandoned and destroyed by the Indians in the winter of 1778-9, located four miles north of Binghamton in Broome County.

12. Choconut, or *Chugnutt*, an important Indian town of fifty or sixty houses mostly on the south side of the Susquehanna River, at the mouth of Big Choconut Creek, in Broome County. Destroyed by General Poor Aug. 19, 1779.

13. Owagea, an Indian town of about twenty houses, on Owego Creek, about a mile from the Susquehanna River, in the north part of present Owego,—was a small hamlet, also near the river. Destroyed August 19, 1779.

14. Manckatawangum, or *Red Bank*,—an Indian town on the south side of the Susquehanna River, nearly opposite the present village of Barton, in Tioga County,—near Fitzgerald's Farm, according to Beatty.

General Sullivan under date of Aug. 30th, says: "The number of Indian towns destroyed since the commencement of the expedition, including those burnt by General Clinton previous to the junction, is, I think, fourteen, some of them considerable, others inconsiderable."

15. Middletown, an Indian hamlet of eight houses, located on the north bank of Chemung River, between Newtown and present Elmira. Destroyed Aug. 31, 1779.

16. Kanawlohalla or *Canaweola*, on the site of present Elmira in Chemung County. George Grant says it contained twenty houses. This was the site of Fort Reid. Destroyed while the army was on the march, August 31, 1779.

17. Big Flats, on the north bank of Chemung River, eight miles above present Elmira. An early French map calls a village at this point Runonvea, Destroyed by a detachment under Colonel Dayton Aug. 31, 1779.

18. Sheoquaga or *Catharine's Town*, an Indian village of thirty houses, located on the site of present Havana in Schuyler County. Destroyed Sept. 2, 1779.

19. Peach Orchard, an Indian town of an unknown name on the site of present Peach Orchard, ten miles north of Havana, on east shore of Seneca lake. Destroyed Sept. 3, 1779.

20. Condawhaw, a small Indian town on the east shore of Seneca lake, at present site of North Hector, so called by Luke Swetland in 1778. Destroyed Sept. 4, 1779.

21. Kendaia, or *Appletown*, located on lot 79, Romulus, on the east side of Seneca lake. It contained about twenty houses. Destroyed Sept. 6, 1779.

22. Butler's Buildings, so called, consisting of a few buildings, located near present canal bridge in the village of Geneva. Destroyed while on the march Sept. 7, 1779.

23. Kanadaseaga, *the grand village*, and capital of the Senecas, located one and a half miles north-west of present Geneva. It contained about sixty well built houses. Destroyed Sept. 9, 1779.

24. Gothseungquean or *Shenanwaga*, a village of twenty houses located on both sides of Kershong Creek, near the west shore of Seneca Lake, seven miles south of Geneva. Destroyed by a detachment under Major Parr, Sept. 8, 1779.

25. Kanandaigua, an Indian town of twenty-three houses, located about a mile from the lake, in west part of present village of Canandaigua. Destroyed Sept. 10, 1779.

26. Hanneyaye, an Indian town of twenty houses, located at foot of Honeoye Lake, east of the outlet. One house was occupied as a fort by Captain Cummings. Destroyed Sept. 11, 1779.

27. Kanaghsaws, also called *Adjutoa*, an Indian town of eighteen houses located three-fourths of a mile south-east of the head of Conesus Lake on the farm of Dr. McMillen. Destroyed September 13, 1779.

28. Gathtsegwarohare or *Cassawauloughly*, an important Indian town of twenty-five houses, located on the east side of Canaseraga Creek, about two miles from its confluence with the Genesee, at the "Hermitage," formerly owned by Judge Caroll. Destroyed Sept. 14, 1779.

29. Chenandoanes or *Great Genesee Castle*, sometimes called Little Beard's Town,—contained one hundred and twenty-eight houses, located on the west side of Genesee river, mostly on the north side of Beard's Creek, north-east of Cuylerville. Destroyed Sept. 15, 1779.

TOWNS DESTROYED BY LIEUTENANT COLONEL BUTLER.

30. Scawyace, or *Long Falls*, an important Indian town on the north bank of the Seneca River on present site of Waterloo, in Seneca County,—was partially destroyed by a volunteer force under Colonel Harper, Sept. 8, 1779,—destruction completed Sept. 21, by Major Scott, of Colonel Butler's detachment.

31. Choharo, a hamlet of two houses at the foot of Cayuga Lake, where Colonel Butler's detachment forded the river. This was the ancient Tichero of the Jesuit Relations. Destroyed Sept. 21, by Colonel Butler.

32. Gewauga, a small hamlet located on the east side of Cayuga Lake, on the site of present Union Springs in Cayuga County. Destroyed Sept. 22, 1779.

33. Goiogouen, of the Jesuit Relations, made up of three separate towns, *viz*:

(*1*). Cayuga Castle, containing fifteen very large houses built of squared logs, located near the south line of the town of Springport in Cayuga County, on the north bank of Great Gully Brook, from one to two miles from the lake.

(*2*). East Cayuga, Old Town, containing thirteen houses, located in the south-east corner of the town of Springport, from three to four miles from Cayuga Lake. A site in the south-west corner of Fleming, was probably a site of this clan. Destroyed Sept. 22.

(*3*). Upper Cayuga, containing fourteen large houses, located near the north line of the town of Ledyard in Cayuga County, on the south bank of Great Gully Brook, from one to two miles from Cayuga Lake. Destroyed Sept. 22.

George Grant describes the three preceding towns as one town containing fifty houses, with many scattering towns within two or three miles. General Sullivan's official report says that "Colonel Butler destroyed five principal towns and a number of scattering houses,—the whole making about one hundred in number." Captain Lodge's Map designates three towns by name.

34. Chonodote or *Peach Tree Town*, also called Chandot, a town containing fourteen houses, located on the site of present Aurora, in

Cayuga County. This town contained 1500 peach trees. Destroyed Sept. 24th by the detachment under Colonel William Butler.

Towns Destroyed by Lieutenant Colonel Dearborn.

35. A small hamlet of three houses, on the Shankwiller farm, in town of Fayette, Seneca County, four miles from Cayuga Lake. Destroyed by Colonel Dearborn Sept. 21..

36. A small town of ten buildings on the west shore of Cayuga lake, one mile north of Canoga Creek. Destroyed by Colonel Dearborn's detachment Sept. 21, 1779.

37. Skannayutenate, an Indian village of ten houses, located on the south bank of Canoga Creek, on the west shore of Cayuga Lake, a half mile north-east of Canoga village in Seneca County. Destroyed by Lieutenant Colonel Dearborn Sept. 21, 1779.

38. Newtown, an Indian village of nine houses, located one mile south-east of village of Canoga, on the west shore of Cayuga Lake, a mile south of Skannayutenate. Destroyed Sept. 21, 1779 by Lieutenant Colonel Dearborn.

39. Swahyawana, an Indian town located on the west shore of Cayuga Lake, on the farm of Edward R. Dean, in the north-east corner of the town of Romulus in Seneca County. Destroyed Sept. 22, 1779, by Lieutenant Colonel Henry Dearborn.

40. Coreorgonel, an important Indian town of twenty-five houses, located on the west side of Cayuga inlet, about two miles south of Ithaca, and three miles from the head of Cayuga Lake. It appears as Todevighrono, the name of the tribe on the Gay Johnson Map of 1771. Destroyed by the detachment under Lieutenant Colonel Dearborn Sept. 24, 1779..

Journal of William McKendry

A lieutenant in the Army of the Revolution and an Original Member of the Society of the Cincinnati of Massachusetts, who died at Canton, Massachusetts, A.D. 1798.

October 25 Colonel Alden drew some cloathing for ye regiment. A cold storm.

October 26 and 27th A cold storm.

October 28th Stormy and obliged to leave ye camp, and go to ye town for shelter in ye rain.

October 29th Stormy, cold and muddy.

October 30th Albany Committee set to provide barracks for General Nixon's Brigade.

October 31st The brigade moved into the town and billited in the houses myself quartered at Mr. Phillip Van Vaiters at ye mill.

1777. *Nov. 1st* Fair and pleasant weather.

November 2, 3, 4 and 5th Nothing worth notice.

November 6th Rainy weather.

November 7, 8 and 9th Nothing worth notice.

November 10th Stormy and cleared off cold the pay master got the money for ye regiment.

November 11th Nothing worth notice.

November 12th Storm of snow.

November 13th. 14, 15 and 16. Nothing new.

November 17th Colonel Alden regiment mustered some squalls of snow and very cold.

November 18, 19, 20 and 21st Nothing new.

November 22nd Bought a horse at publick vendue in Albany gave £13.7.0 £ money.

November 23, 24, 25 and 26 Nothing new.

November 27th Lieutenant Steel died and was buried 28th *ditto*.

November 29th A cold storm hail snow and rain.

November 30th Nothing new.

December 1st 1777. I moved to Mr Henrick R. Lansing near ye. City Hall.

December 2, 3, 4 and 5th Cold.

December 6th Ensign Dewey died of the small pox, very cold.

December 7th General Gates ordered one half gill of rum to be delivered per man per day until farther orders.

December 8th Nothing new.

December 9th Some soldiers ordered to Schenactide to have the smallpox.

December 10th Sent ye horses into ye country to be kept by general orders.

December 11, 12, 13,. 14, 15, 16 and 17th Nothing new.

December 18th Thanksgiving at Albany.

December 19, 20, 21, 22nd Nothing new.

December 23rd Received two waggoners to ride wood for Colonel Alden's regiment.

December 24, 25, 26th Nothing new.

December 27th Lieutenant Buffinton arrived at Albany from home.

December 28, 29th Nothing new.

December 30th General Gates left Albany for ye Southard very cold weather.

December 31st Lieutenant Larry tryed at a general court marshall for selling soldier's clothing and was broke.

January 1st 1778 Adjutant White left Albany on furlow for Springfield.

January 2nd A man was taken up and put into ye City Hall on suspicion of killing a man for his money, after found guilty and was hanged—a thaw.

Ditto 3rd Colonel Alden's Regiment musterd, Ensign Pike arrived in camp from furlow.

January 4th Nothing new.

January 5th Captain Ballard left Albany on furlow for home.

January 6, 7, 8, 9th Nothing new.

January 10th Mr. Elijah Tolman was appointed to command Captain Lanes' company.

January 11th 1778. Moderate snowstorm.

January 12th T. Taylor received 400 lashes for striking Captain Toogood with his gun; he belongs to Colonel Putman's Regiment.

January 13, 14, 15, 16, 17, 18, 19, 20th Nothing new.

January 21st Colonel Alden drew one week's forrage for his horse in Albany.

January 22nd, 23rd Nothing new.

January 24th Colonel Stacy arrived in camp from furlow.

January 25, 26, 27th Nothing new.

January 28th Major Whitting left Albany on furlow for New England.

January 29th Nothing new.

January 30th Captain Day and Captain Warren arrived in camp in Albany with ye clothing for ye officers; Sargeant Dickerman and Corporal Pettingill arrived *ditto*.

January 31st Colonel Greaton and Quarter Master M'Mish left Albany for New England Colonel Alden took ye command . . . a snowstorm.

February 1st 1778. Ensign Parker arrived from furlow at Albany.

February 2nd Nothing new.

February 3rd Captain Coburn left Albany on furlow for New England.

February 4th Nothing New.

February 5th Colonel Alden's regiment mustered.

February 6th A Brittish soldier received thirty lashes at ye City Hall in Albany put on by an Indian.

February 7th A smart snowstorm.

February 8th Nothing new.

February 9th Colonel Alden left Albany on furlow for New England.

February 10th Nothing new.

February 11th Snowstorm cleared of with rain.

February 12, 13, 14, 15, 16, 17th Nothing new.

February 18th Received a letter from New England from Captain Crane.

February 19th The troops reviewed by General De la Fyatt from France.

February 20th, 21st, 22nd, 23rd, 24th Nothing new.

February 25th Captain Partrick arrived at Albany from furlow.

February 26th, 27th Nothing new.

February 28th General Arnold left Albany for ye southard to his home he not being able for ye field by reason of his late wound in his leg—Lieutenant Buffinton left Albany on furlow for New England.

March 1, 2, 3, 4th 1778 Nothing new.

March 5th I left Albany on furlow for New England after going by the way of Hartford arrived ye 10th at Stoughton. Left Stoughton 18th April 1778 after going by ye way of Hartford, Newhaven Fish Kills arrived at Albany 23rd instant 6 o'clock p. m. at Mr. Lansing—Nothing in this time worth entering.

April 24, 25, 26th 1778 Nothing new.

April 27th Marched from Albany for ye northward Colonel Greaton's regiment and Colonel Alden's arrived at half-moon General Conway commanded.

April 28, 29, 30th Quartered at half moon the alarm from the northard was false.

May 1st 1778. Marched from half-moon back for Albany and arrived 4 o'clock p. m.

From the 2nd to ye 13th Nothing new.

May 14th Colonel Alden's regiment mustered, a great day of rejoicing at Albany for the news received from France fired 52 cannon 3 vollies from small arms General Conway had the command.

May 15th There was two men hanged at Albany one for murder the other for robbery the troops was under arms.

May 16, 17, 18, 19, 20th Nothing new.

May 21st Colonel Greaton arrived at Albany from furlow.

May 22nd. Colonel Greatons regiment imbarked for the high lands and left Albany.

May 23, 24, 25, 26, 27, 28, 29th Nothing new.

May 30th Saturday Captain Partrick and Lieutenant Maynard with a number of troops from Colonel Alden's regiment attacked a number of Indians commanded by one Brant at Covers Kill 59 miles S. West from Albany 12 o'clock a. m. with Captain Partrick one lieutenant one serjeant one drum one fife 29 Soldiers—six militia was killed one captain 15 continental—two militia—three wounded—Lieutenant Maynard and three more were taken.

June 1st 1778. Nothing new.

June 2nd Colonel Alden's regiment mustered Albany the Militia were ordered under arms at this place for fear of the Tories rising.

June 3rd Captain Partrick and ye men killed with him were buried by ye Militia.

June 4th Nothing new.

June 5th Seven men were hanged at Albany all for robbery one Rogers and —— in ye number.

June 6th Captain Partrick's cloathing was sold at vendue in Albany amount £64 15 0 £ money Lieutenant Maynard sold *ditto*.

June 7, 8, 9, 10th Nothing new.

June 11th 1778 Colonel Alden's regiment under marching orders left ye barracks and was ordered to be searched for Indian silver, ordered to return into ye barracks again.

June 12, 13, 14, 15, 16, 17, 18, 19, 20, 21st Nothing new.

June 22nd Captain Day left Albany on command.

June 23rd Nothing new.

June 24th Captain Ballard Lieutenant Buffinton left Albany for Cognawagna and with them two serjeants two drummers and fife 42 rank and file.—Proceeded as far as Cherry Valley 70 miles west from Albany with them Comy Woodman. Captain Reed arrived from furlow at this place.

June 25, 26, 27, 28, 29, 30th Very warm weather.

July 1, 2, 3, 4, 5, 6, 7, 8th Warm thunder and showers.

July 9th Colonel Alden's regiment mustered, turned out and took Colonel Weelock's regiment for refusing their duty.

July 10th Colonel Alden's regiment received orders to march for Fort Stannix according to orders proceeded as far as Jacob Truaxes cripple bush eleven miles from Albany.

July 11th arrived at Schenactida 9 o'clock a. m. five miles from Truaxes, lodged at John Babtist. Van Eps Junior twenty-six miles from Albany ten miles from Schenactida lost the horses of ye regiment and found them 10 o'clock a. m.

July 12th Dined at Sir John Johnston's on Mohawk River lodged at Major Funday's in Cognawagna had a Dutch preist to pray with us and was much scared—seventeen miles from Van Eps.

July 13th Dined at Mr. M'Kennys lodged at Major Yates twelve miles from Major Funday's in Conny Joharrow Mohawk River.

July 14th Dined at Major Yates set off from Major Yates 4 o'clock p. m. Captain Ballard joined ye regiment from Cherry Valley lodged at Peter Wormwoods Palatina four miles from Major Yates.

July 15th Marched and crossed ye ferry four miles from said Wormwood's 8 o'clock a. m. breakfast at Coonel Clocks 11 o'clock a. m. arrived at King Henricks Fort drinked some grog in his pallace went into the block houses marched from said pallace and stopped at Peter Digerts and drinkt some grog half a mile from General Hercamons Farm dined at Mr. Walter Digerts nine miles from Colonel Clocks. Crossed ye ferry two miles from Walter Digerts at the Little Falls lodged. at John Peteries opposite Colonel Bellens at said little carrying place, fifteen miles from Wormwoods.

July 16th Marched from said Petries and forded ye river arrived at ye German flats 8 o'clock a. m. at Fort Dayton seven miles from said Petries. Drew provisions at said fort for one day. Dined in the woods one mile from said fort—Marched and made a small halt at Germintown Fort lodged at Mr. Thompsons ten miles from Fort Dayton— seventeen miles from Little falls—no inhabitants living at said Thompsons. Captain Ballard's cow broke her leg.

July 17th Marched from said Thompsons, and crossed ye river at Fort Schyler made a halt, and, eat some dinner marched to Areseo[1] fields an Indian town and incampt by ye river twelve miles from Thompsons.

July 18th Marched from Areseo fields 6. o'clock a. m. and arrived

---

1. The original seems to be thus; but the name is Areseo or Aresca, usually given Oreska or Oreske.—J. W.

at Fort Stannix 9 o'clock a. m. Encampt below ye fort, set up our huts with boards dined with the Major on fresh sammon—eight miles from Areseo fields:

July 19th Raised my tent. Colonel Stacy moved out of ye fort into his Markee.

July 20th Drew two days provision a large quantity of fresh sammon brought to this fort by the Indians six shillings per sammon L money—An express arrived from the southard another from Albany with orders from General Starks for Colonel Stacy to march his regiment to Cherry Valley.

July 21st Marched from Fort Stannix 10 o'clock a. m. arrived at Areseo Fields, 12, a. m. marched on and crossed ye creek near Fort Scyler and waited some hours for the *bateau*. Lodged at said Thompsons mentioned going up.

July 22nd Marched from said Thompsons and lodged at John Petries at ye little carrying place mentioned in my going up.

July 23 Marched from said Petries took twelve Indians which had ben plundering ye inhabitants brought them by Colonel Stacy's order to Colonel Clocks dined at said Clocks lodged at Major Yates *palatina* went to Stone Robby for a bullock to kill for ye regiment to Captain Tigerts.

July 24th Marched from Major Yates and arrived at Cherry Valley 4 o'clock p. m. had some [*blank*] Had a heavy rain the regiment was received with much joy with firing a blunderbuss and one round from the militia and inhabitants which were posted at Cherry Valley the first friend that offered to me was John Woodman aforesaid at said post.

July 25th Drew two days provisions and went to the Reverend Mr. Dunlaps and drank Sillabub with discoursing the old gentleman about sundries affairs.

Ditto 26th Sunday went to Church—Text 1st Samuel 12 verse Mr. Johnston Chaplain—Colonel Stacy received a letter from General Starks.

Great encouragement that his regiment should not want for anything that lay in his power to help them to.

July 27th Mowed and raked one hour for Robert Wills, Colonel Stacy, Adjutant White *ditto*—Began to board with Mr. James Richey twenty rods from Fort Alden.

July 28th Heavy rain.

July 29th Captain Lane arrived at Cherry Valley.

July 30th Colonel Alden arrived at this place Paymaster Hickling *ditto*—Commissary Smith of Bay stores *ditto*—two pieces of cannon.

July 31st Had a high corus stampt hats fired a cannon made an alarm.

August 1st 1778 Brought my horse from Mr. Richey's pasture.

August 2nd Sunday, Attended publick worship in Fort Alden.

August 3rd Went to John Campbell's and viewed some horses drank some cyder supt with Lieutenant Lunt and lodged at Mr. Dunlap's.

August 4th Mr. Aaron Thompson liked to ben killed breaking a colt.

August 5th Lost my horse—Captain Ballard arrived from scout the troops moved from Colonel Campbell's to the fort.

August 6th Mr. Richey moved from Cherry Valley for Albany for fear of the enemy.

August 7th Began to build the redout at Fort Alden.

August 8th Went to the beaver dam to Mr. Harper's saw mill for boards—Sent my horse to ye beaver dam to pasture to Mr. Hammells.

August 9th Captain Lane joined ye company mess at Mr. Richey's.

August 10th Pleasant weather.

August 11th Captain Ballard arrived at Lieutenant Campbell's from ye Butter-nuts went to Mr. Ramsies and drank milk punch with Captain Parker and Commissary Woodman.

August 12th Captain Ballard arrived from a scout at Cherry Valley brought in with him from ye Butter-nuts 73 head of horn cattle 40 Sheep 14 Horses 14 Tories.

August 13th Captain Ballard set out for Albany with a guard and ye Tories.

August 14th Rode to ye beaver dam and saw mill with Colonel Stacy.

August 15th Fort Alden was named by Captain Hickling went in ye evening to Colonel Alden's quarters and drank milk punch.

August 16th Colonel Whelock arrived from a scout from Unadilla.

August 17th Lieutenant Holden and Lieutenant Carter arrived at

Cherry Valley.

August 18th Lieutenant Holden began to board at Mr. Richeys.

August 19th Commissary Smith left Cherry Valley after more stores.

August 20, 21, 22nd Nothing new.

August 23rd Colonel Stacy arrived from scout informed us that one of our men killed an Indian, which proved true.

August 24th Lieutenant Trowbridge arrived at Cherry Valley.

August 25th Went to Colonel Campbell's and se ye Dominies bee wool breaking.

August 26th Went to Harmony Hall and drank some grog.

August 27th Went to the beavers dam on horseback with all the field officers, had a high corus running horses.

August 28, 29, 30th Some rain.

August 31st Went to Major Clydes.

September 1st 1778 Nothing new.

September 2nd Commissary Woodman went to Stone Robby Captain Lane went to the Salt Spring.

September 3rd Nothing new.

September 4th Captain Ballard arrived from Albany, Lieutenant Bratt wounded an Indian.

September 5th Commissary Woodman arrived from the river.

September 6th Nothing new.

September 7th Went to Harmony Hall.

September 8th Sent to Albany for ye baggage of the regiment.

September 9th Captain McKeen arrived from scout fired some guns at the Beaver Dam, alarmed the camp detachment a party from the fort marched one mile and found it to be a false alarm—returned to the fort again—Captain McKeen brought in three prisoners from Unadilla.

September 10th, 11th Nothing new.

September 12th Rain and cold for ye season.

September 13th Nothing new.

September 14th Captain Ballard's Tory stock sold at vendue.

September 15th The baggage arrived from Albany for the regiment.

September 16th Nothing new.

September 17th Alarm Brant with a party of Indians and Tories burnt German flats 44 houses 44 barns killed three men, drove off 90 head of Continental fat cattle besides those took from the inhabitants a large number burnt grane without measure, a detachment from Colonel Alden's regiment under the command of Major Daniel Whitting pursued them but without much success being detained by one cowardly Colonel Clock—The major brought in three of their men prisoners which were taken under arms.

September 18th Colonel Clock arrived at Mount Moore four miles from this garrison and returned back by reason of and false alarm made by the Tories at Mohawk River.

September 19, 20th Nothing new.

September 21st Major Whitting returned from scout with three prisoners mentioned above.

September 22nd, 23rd Nothing new.

September 24th Commissary Smith arrived at Cherry Valley with Bay Stores.

September 25th Colonel Alden's regiment mustered at Cherry Valley the regiment was arranged.

September 26th Lieutenant Holden moved from Mr Richey's to Colonel Campbell's.

September 27th Lieutenant Benjamin Billing left Cherry Valley for home by reason of dissatisfaction in the rank of ye regiment.

September 28th Nothing new.

September 29th Rode towards Springfield with the commissary. Stopped at Mr. Culley's heavy rain.

September 30th Captain Hickling left Cherry Valley after money for the regiment—Brought my horse from ye Beaver Dam.

October 1778 *1, 2, 3, 4th* Nothing new.

October 5th Mr. Richey arrived at Cherry Valley from Albany.

October 6th Colonel Stacy and Captain Ballard had a horse race Colonel Stacy won the bet.

October 7t 8, 9, 10, 11, 12, 13, 14th Nothing new.

October 15th Went to the Salt Springs in ye evening wet my appointment wine . . 28 . . dollars.

October 16th Lieutenant William White wet his appointment in Mr. Richey's with wine amount 36 dollars.

October 17, 18, 19, 20th Nothing new.

October 21st Rode out to Springfield with the commissary and Mr. Witter Johnston six miles from Cherry Valley.

October 22nd Rode to Dominies Johnston's in company with Captain Reed and Commissary Woodman to the wedding of Captain McKeen and Mrs. Jenny Campbell.

October 23rd Serjeant Elijah Dickerman and Letty Gibbens was married at the house of James Richey; in Cherry Valley. By the Reverend Mr. Johnston late of Tunadilla drank seven gallons wine.

October 24th Nothing new.

October 25th Commissary Smith left Cherry Valley.

October 26th Had a field day fired six rounds per man.

October 27th Colonel Alden left Cherry Valley for Albany.

October 28, 29, 30, 31st Nothing new.

November 1st 1778 Some snow at this place.

November 2nd, 3rd Nothing new.

November 4th Captain Hickling arrived at Cherry Valley with money for ye regiment.

November 5, 6, 7, 8, 9, 10th. Nothing new.

November 11th Alarm 11. o' clock a. m. Mr. Hammell coming from the Beaver Dam, was fired uppon by ye Indians and was wounded he being on horse rode off and got clear it being half a mile from the fort: he rode to Colonel Alden's quarters and informed him of the matter—Immediately came on 442 Indians from the five Nations 200 Tories under the command of one Colonel Butler and Captain Brant, attacked headquarters killed Colonel Alden took Colonel Stacy prisoner attacked Fort Alden after three hours retreated without success of taking the fort killed of the regiment 14 men names (*viz.*)

Ichabod Alden	Thomas Holden
Robert Henderson	Daniel Dudley
Thomas Sheldon	Enos Blakeley
Gideon Day	Thomas Noles
Benjamin Worsley	Oliver Deball
Pet. Adams	Simeon Hopkins

Thoma Mires   Robert Bray.[2]

November 11th Took prisoners from ye regiment William Stacy, Lieutenant Colonel Aaron Holden, Lieutenant Andrew Garret ,Ensign Suzer De Beaver, Surgeon Mate, 11 soldiers their names not mentioned.

Killed of ye inhabitants 30 persons
took of ,,   *ditto*   34 *ditto*
Wounded 2 *ditto* one of the Regiment
Burnt—20 houses 25 Barns 2 Mills
N. B. a rainy day.

November 12th Sent out and fetched in Colonel Alden and buried him under arms with firing three vollies over his grave—Brant came with 100 Indians 8 o'clock a. m. to attack ye fort ye second time but receiving two or three shots from the cannon gave back left ye fort 3 o'clock p. m. Brought in a number of the dead bodies.

November13th. Colonel Clock arrived at Fort Alden 12 o'clock a.m. after a long cowardly march of twelve miles with 400 men left ye fort in about one hour and marched back for Mohawk River— Brought in Huew Mitchal's wife and four children all dead and scalpt with a number of other dead bodies.

November 14th An express arrived from Colonel Butler Commanding at Schoharrow that he was advancing with 500 men to ye relief of Fort Alden—Snow rain.

November 15th A heavy snow storm fell two feet deep.

November 16th found Captain Scott's wife dead and was buried.

November 17th An express arrived from Schoharrow.

November 18th Nothing new.

November 19th Very cold and blustering.

November 20th Lieutenant Trowbridge set out for Albany Captain Ballard found two barrels of cyder.

November 21st Nothing new.

November 22nd Alarm said that the Indians was discovered at Mr. Culley's detachment out a party from Colonel Alden's regiment and marched to said Culleys and the Indians turned out to be our own men.

---

2. The name of James Parmineter is erased.

November 23rd, 24th, 25th Nothing new.

November 26th Thanksgiving at this place, found one of our men dead and was buried killed by ye Indians in the 11th.

November 27th Nothing new.

November 28th The muster master and pay master arrived at Cherry Valley with the cloathing for the regiment, it was very good.

November 29th The late Colonel Alden's regiment mustered by Captain Lush in Fort Alden, one man died of his wound received in the action of ye 11th instant.

November 30th Cold and blustering.

December 1st, 2nd Nothing new.

December 3rd Captain Warren, Lieutenant Thorp, Lieutenant Curtis, left Cherry Valley on furlow for New England.

December 4th Lieutenant Trowbridge left camp for Albany.

December 5th John Stacy began to live with me.

December 6, 7, 8, 9th Nothing new.

December 10th Snowstorm twelve inches deep

December 11th Received three letters from Stoughton by ye hand of Corporal Hewins.

December 12th, 13th Nothing new.

December 14th Captain Reed, Lieutenant Lunt, Lieutenant Givins, left camp in cherry valley on furlow for New England.

December 15, 16, 17, 18th Nothing new.

December 19th Pay Master Tucker arrived at Cherry Valley with two months pay.

December 20th Very warm for the season.

December 21st Began to snow.

December 22nd, 23rd, 24th Nothing new.

December 25th Major Daniel Whitting and Paymaster Tucker, left Cherry Valley for Boston after clothing for ye officers.

December 26, 27, 28, 29, 30, 31st Nothing new.

1779. *January 1, 2, 3, 4, 5, 6th* Nothing new.

January 7th The late Colonel Alden's regiment was mustered by Colonel Varrack at Cherry Valley.

January 8th William Hancock received 100 lashes for theft—Captain Lane arrested for affronting Captain Ballard.

January 9th Began to snow. Commissary Woodman arrived from ye river.

January 10, 11, 12, 13, 14th Nothing new.

January 15th Captain Lane Mr. Johnston and Mr. Richey left Cherry Valley for Albany.

January 16, 17th Nothing new.

January 18th Went to Newtown Martin and bought two stacks of hay from James Bradshaw ye weather very cold.

January 19, 20, 21st Nothing new.

January 22nd Serjeant Dickerman with his wife left Cherry Valley for Stoughton, had leave of absence for thirty days.

January 23rd, 24, 25th Nothing new.

January 26th Set out with eleven officers of the late Colonel Alden's regiment for Fort Plank for the tryal of Captain Lane dined at Fort Plank lodged at Goshen Van Alstines on Mohawk River.

January 27th Waited on the court marshall at Mr. Severs in *pallatina* dined *ditto*—Arrived at Fort Alden 9 o'clock p. m.

January 28th, 29th Nothing new.

January 30th Received a quantity of camp equipage from Colonel Lewin [Lewis?] in Albany.

January 31st Cold and blustering.

February 1st 1779 Cold.

February 2nd Found Simeon Hopkins dead in ye woods who was killed in the action of the 11th November last and was buried at this garrison.

February 3rd Heavy rain and thaw.

February 4th Very cold and froze hard.

February 5th Very cold and blustering with snow and wind.

February 6th Captain Ballard sent out a scout consisting of seventeen men commanded by Lieutenant Day to proceed as far as Lake Otsago fifteen miles.

February 7th Lieutenant Day returned without making any discoveries of ye enemy.

February 8th Nothing new.

February 9th Major Whitting arrived from furlow at Cherry Valley.

February 10th Lieutenant Trowbridge arrived from Albany the weather warm.

February 11th Cold and froze hard Lieutenant Carter began to bile sugar at Cherry Valley.

February 12th Left Fort Alden with Doctor Brown 2 o'clock p.m. and rode to Bowman's Creek five miles, drank tea at Mr. Wills—Serjeant Hunter arrived at said Wills from Schoharrow lately deserted from ye Indians 60 miles below Ocquaugo.—Gave us an account that he left them 25th January 1779, and another man with him said Hunter was taken on a scout 10th November 1778 ye day before ye destruction of Cherry Valley—Informs that he was seven days in the woods with little or no provisions—Informs that the last he knew of Colonel Stacy he was well and in good spirits; and told him not to mind it for it was only the fortune of war—Colonel Stacy was in the hands of Colonel Butler, and that the French doctor was not very well—Says that only one of his party was killed when he was taken, one Robert Bray when he ran from the Indian he brought off one brass kettle and axe which he supposed much affronted ye Indians as they set much by them, further says not. I bought 25 skipples of pees from Mr. Lyon afterward returned to Fort Alden 9 o'clock p. m. two small scout sent from Fort Alden, returned without making any discoveries.

February 13th Went into ye woods with Captain Lane to tap sugar trees, katched eight palefulls—a small scout went out this day from Fort Alden returned without making any discoveries.

February 14th Sunday.—Rainy weather orders came from General Clinton for two companies to be detached from Fort Alden and sent to Fort Hercamin.

February 15th Rode to Bowman's Creek for waggons to carry ye baggage—Captain Lanes sentance read on ye parade and cleared from his arrest.

February 16th 11 o'clock a. m. Captain Coburn marched from Fort Alden for Fort Hercamin; with one captain lieutenant two subs: six serjeants six corporals four drummers and fife rank and file.

February 17th An express arrived from Fort Plank to Fort Alden informs with two letters from Onida that ye Indians were on their march, but to what part they could not say.

February 18th The inhabitants began to move into Fort Alden for fear of the Indians—Some snow and rain.

February 19th Some rain Pay Master Tucker wrote to Major Whitting and informed him that he was at Mohawk River, with the money for the regiment and wanted orders to proceed which were granted.

February 20th Paymaster Tucker arrived at Cherry Valley with two months' pay for the regiment.

February 21st Paid the regiment &c.

February 22nd Paymaster left Fort Alden for Fort Hercamin.

February 23rd The weather cool—was informed that Colonel Gansworth's regiment was on their march up Mohawk River.
Cold and blustering.

February 25th Adjutant White left Fort Alden for Albany for a furlow.

February 26th Snow and rain moved from the meeting house into ye block house west-end of the fort with Captain Lane and the commissary—Mr. Culley's familey moved from Fort Alden to ye Mohawk River.

February 27th Lieutenant Curtis and Lieutenant Thorp arrived at Fort Alden from furlow received three letters from Stoughton.

February 28th An express arrived from Fort Plank and informs that two scout of the Indians were out eighteen days and where destined they could not tell one of 80 the other 100 men.

March 1st 1779. Captain B. Warren, arrived at Fort Alden from furlow.

March 2nd Pleasant weather &c.

March 3rd Made sugar troughs and katched some sap.

March 4th An express arrived from Fort Plank at Fort Alden informs, that the enemy was on their move and was supposed that the Mohawk River was their object the intelligence came by two Indians from Niaugary sent an express from Fort Alden to Schoharrow to inform them of the matter.

March 5th Snowed very fast this day.

March 6th Some snow—William Hancock received 100 lashes for theft—The late Colonel Alden's regiment mustered in Fort Alden by Mr. Lush D. M. master.

March 7th Sunday. Some snow.

March 8th Dull weather went to William Shanklin's and brought in some oats.

March 9th Some snow—brought some hay from Newtown Martin.

March 10th Rode to Bowman's Creek with Doctor Brown to purchase oats and purchased 40 skipples—Dined at Mr. Hickey's returned to Fort Alden.

March 11th Thunder and lightening some snow.

March 12th Snowy day—Sent to Bowman's Creek for oats.

March 13th Colonel Clyde and Doctor Younglove arrived at Fort Alden.

March 14th Sunday—Snowed this day—Eleven nine-months men discharged from Fort Alden.

March 15th Cold and clear for the season.

March 16th Nothing new.

March 17th Captain Tilman arrived at Fort Alden from Albany.

March 8th Clear and cool &c.

March 19th Some snow—Captain Day arrived at Fort Alden from furlow.

March 20th Left Fort Alden with Commissary Woodman—crossed Mohawk River at Goshen Van Alstines dined five miles west from Major Fundars lodged at Sir William Castle.

March 21st Sunday. Left Sir William Castle and dined at Schenectady at Mr. Johnstons—Snowed in the afternoon arrived at Albany at Mr. Henry R. Lansings 5 o'clock, p. m.

March 22nd Snowed in the morning—saw Lieutenant Lunt—arrived from furlow.

March 23rd Lieutenant Peebody left Albany on furlow—drank some punch at Captain Bogerts with Colonel Lewis and Mr. Lansing.

March 24th Snowy day. A man was found dead between Albany and Schenectady in the highway.

March 25th Snowy day and dull weather.

March 26th and *27th* Nothing new.

March 28th Sunday—Pleasant weather went to church to hear Mr. Levingston.

March 29th Left Albany with Commissary Woodman 9 o'clock a.

m. Dined at Schenectidy and lodged at Sir William Castle.

March 30th Left Sir William Castle 8 o'clock a. m.—dined at Master Van Alstines—arrived at Fort Alden 6 o'clock p. m . Snow three feet deep.

March 31st Pleasant weather billed 16 lb sugar.

April 1st 1779. Pleasant warm. Snow two feet deep in Cherry Valley.

April 2nd Pleasant weather snow went off fast.

April 3rd Sultry hot thunder and showers.

April 4th Sunday. Captain Day left Fort Alden, for Fort Hercamin to take the command there; Snow all gone.

April 5th Fort Alden alarmed fired two cannon it was said that some Indians was discovered at the Beaver Dam but turned out to be a false alarm one of the soldiers killed a wolf.

April 6th Some snow and rain, cool weather Serjeant Smith arrived from furlow in Fort Alden.

April 7th Pleasant weather.

April 8th This day orders came to Fort Alden for a detachment to march to Fort Schyler.

April 9th Captain Lane marched from Fort Alden for Fort Schyler with two subs three serjeants 43 corporals, 52 rank and file.

April 10th Pleasant and warm.

April 11th Sunday—The guard mounted with serjeant and corporals only in Fort Alden to spell the men duty so hard.

April 12th Weather cool and some rain.

April 13th This day Fort Plank alarmed fired three cannon some Indians seen back of Johnston and took six prisoners by waylaying ye road one of them escaped

April 14, 15, 16 and 17th Nothing remarkable some snow fell.

April 18th Sunday—cool and snowstorm.

April 19th Some snow fell Serjeant Wright returned from Albany.

April 20th Pleasant weather—made in my mess this spring 168 pounds of maple sugar in Cherry Valley.

April 21st This day was informed that one man was killed in Stone Arabia by the Indians and five prisoners taken above Fort Plank.

April 22nd This day was informed that a captain of Militia in Tille Barrack back of Stone Arabia with six men fought ye Indians ye captain lost two men and killed four Indians ye captain's wife was wounded—his son killed.

Three Indians discovered on Brimstone Hill by one of the inhabitants.

April 23rd This day Ira Johnston arrived in Fort Alden, ran from the Indians he was taken 11th November last in Cherry Valley the way he left them was, he had been 150 miles twice last winter for corn for the Indians and carried one bushel on his back said way—the 3rd time came for corn within twenty miles of the Onida Castle where Continental troops were stationed—in the night ran from the Indian that he was with and reached Onida Castle was followed by ye Indian but not overtaken—from said castle came to Fort Schyler, from that to Fort Alden—informed us that Colonel Stacy, Lieutenant Holden and Ensign Garrett was all well the last he had heard from them the rest of the prisoners were scattered among ye Indians.

April 24th Serjeant Merrill returned from furlow at Fort Alden.

April 25th Sunday. Pleasant weather.

April 26th Bought a horse in Cherry Valley gave 105 dollars for him.

April 27th Pleasant weather.

April 28th. Some showers, Froze hard in the night.

April 29th This day Captain Lane arrived in Fort Alden from his scout informs that he had been with a party under the command of Colonel Van Scoik and cut of three Indian castles at Onidauga [killed] 60 took 33 prisoners, burnt 47 houses and large quantities of corn not one of the party killed.

April 30th Some rain and some snow—cold for the season &c.

May 1st Pleasant weather—Nothing new.

May 2nd (Sunday) This day a man arrived at Fort Alden ran from the Indians was taken about a month ago, above Fort Plank near Mohawk River he informs that Butler is out with a party of Indians, the late prisoner has ben eight days without any food excepting roots that he gathered on his way.

May 3rd Pleasant weather—This day sent our horses to pasture some showers in the afternoon.

May 4th The late Colonel Alden's regiment mustered by Captain Lush—Captain Reed arrived at Fort Alden from furlow Lieutenant Buffinton Lieutenant Givins, gone to Fort Hercamin.

May 5th Captain Ballard and Captain Bogert from Albany went to the foot of Lake Otsago, to look out a good landing for the stores to be sent to that place some squalls of snow today.

May 6th Cool weather for the season.

May 7th Doctor Brown and Pay Master Tucker arrived from Albany at Fort Alden.

May 8th Pay Master began to pay the regiment.

May 9th Sunday. Pleasant weather John Tolman arrived at Fort Alden from Stoughton.

May 10th Pleasant weather &c.

May 11th P. m. left Fort Alden for Fort Hercamin.

May 12th This day was informed that at the great flats a few days agone was killed and scalped two men and three women one woman taken prisoner, two women more were scalped and are yet alive all done by the Indians.

May 13th Some rain and cool.

May 14th This day was informed that a large number of Indians was discovered not far from Fort Plank—a scout ordered with four days' provisions from Fort Alden—tomorrow to make discoveries—the people left Bowman s Creek—two families moved to Fort Alden.

May 15th Ensign Parker arrived at Fort Alden from Fort Hercamin from his command.

May 16th (Sunday) Lieutenant Carter left Fort Alden with the regemental return for Albany—Some of the enemy discovered near this garrison this evening.

May 17th 3 o'clock this morning the centry discharged his piece at a man that was making towards him the garrison was alarmed and manned the lines, the enemy was discovered no more at this time—Lieutenant Lunt was appointed to do the duty of an adjutant.

May 18th Some rain and cloudy dark weather.

May 19th This morning 9 o'clock. I left Fort Alden with Lieutenant Day and Commissary Woodman for Mohawk River after flour for the garrison—dined at Goshen Van. Alstines. Some rain this day.

May 20th Left the river 2 o'clock p. m. Rained very hard. Arrived at Fort Alden 6 o'clock p m. was very wet.

May 21st Some rain this morning.

May 22nd . Captain Lane and Lieutenant Curtis ran a race Captain Lane was beat.

May 23rd (Sunday) Very pleasant this day.

May 24th Pinkster day among the Dutch.

May 25th Colonel Clyde arrived at Fort Alden—informs that Colonel Gansworts regiment was on their march up Mohawk River.

May 26th Some rain this day, sold my two horses for 750 dollars Lieutenant Carter arrived from Albany.

May 27th This afternoon about 7 o'clock three men was discovered within musket shot of this garrison the centry fired on them they made to the bush and were seen no more the lines were manned we supposed them to be spies.

May 28th This day three men were discovered again near the garrison, Serjeant Clerk fired his rifle at them they made off—sent a party of men after them, but could not overtake them.

May 29th Adjutant White arrived. in Fort Alden from Boston with the gratuity money for some of ye men.

May 30 (Sunday) Went out as far as Mr. Larklins with Doctor Brown and Commissary Woodman to view that part of the town.

May 31st Sent the baggage of the regiment to Albany agreeable to the generals orders—Serjeant Cutting, Serjeant Connant with two French recruits arrived in Fort Alden—A man was shot in Albany this day.—Adjutant set out for Fort Herkimen.

June 1st Lieutenant Day left Fort Alden for Albany on command, Adjutant White returned from Fort Hercamin.

June 2nd Cool weather for the season—This day was informed not many days agone six Indians took two men prisoners from turlough [sic] (twelve miles from Fort Alden) carried them as far as Ocquaugo where two of the Indians left the party to go on to inform their brothers of their success, when the four that was left got asleep the two prisoners took their hatchets and killed two of the Indians the other two awoke and started the white men being two ready for them wounded them both and the two Indians fled, the two late prisoners took the Indian's arms of the dead and those that had fled with only their lives,

113

and made their escape—the Indians soon were alarmed in that quarter and came to the ground, set the woods all on fire, so that they might discover their tracks that had made their escape, but to no purpose the two late English prisoners escaped clear—I have had the pleasure since to see the man that killed the two Indians it was Mr. Sawyer.

June 3rd A very hard frost last night which killed the blossoms at this place.

June 4th This morning 2 o'clock this garrison was alarmed the centry had fired on a man that was creeping towards him but soon ran off and was discovered no more the lines were manned .

June 5th Pay Master Tucker arrived in Fort Alden with cloathing for the regiment informs that the British troops has got to the highlands above N.York Lieutenant Peebody arrived in Fort Alden from furlow.

June 6th (Sunday) Lieutenant Day arrived in Fort Alden from Albany.

June 7th Pay Master Tucker gave out the cloathing to the regiment in this garrison.

June 8th. Pay Master Tucker left Fort Alden with cloathing for the men at Fort Hercamin.

June 9th Warm and showry.

June 10th This day the centry discovered a man creeping towards the wood choppers centry fired on him he was seen no more.

June 11th Cold weather for the season.

June 12th A scout was ordered from Fort Alden, returned without making any discoveries of the enemy.

June 13 (Sunday) Heavy rain,—this day was informed—that some days agone the Indians took six prisoners from Germantown above German-Flatts and let one of them return which was an old woman.

June 14th This day orders came to Major Whiting from General Clinton, for the regiment to hold themselves in readiness to march at an hour's warning and General Clinton was to make his headquarters in Cennagoharry for a few days.

June 15th The provisions in Fort Alden all condemned Commissary Woodman went to Mohawk River after provisions for the garrison.

June 16th Major Whiting received a letter from General Clinton to wait on him at the river. Commissary Woodman arrived from said river.

June 17th Major Whiting and Adjutant White went to the river and returned with orders for the Regiment to march tomorrow for Lake Otsago.

June 18th The regiment marched from Fort Alden (in Cherry Valley) 11 o'clock a. m. encampt this night in Springfield six miles from the fort. Major Whiting ordered a fatiguing party on to mend the roads towards the lake it was commanded by Captain Ballards.

June 19th The regiment marched from Springfield with eight waggons carrying the baggage 12 o'clock a. m. Arrived at Lake Otsago 3 o'clock p. m: Captain Lane had gone forward to clear the encampment—Encampt on the heights five miles march this day.

June 20th (Sunday) Cleared the passage for the waggons to unload the stores—60 *batteaus* arrived at this lake and a quantity of provisions from the river.

June 21st The Light Infantry company and late Colonel Alden's joined the regiment at this place from Fort Hercamin— party of men was ordered by Colonel Butler to the foot of the lake to dam the same that the water might be raised to carry the boats currant down Susquehanna-River—Captain Warren Six Masts. Regiment commanded the party—This day a man was hanged at Mohawk River taken up for a spy that was viewing the stores as they passed up the river he informed General Clinton that he was a lieutenant in Butler service which is now with the Indians also informs that another Tory and nine Indians came off with him.

June 22nd The late Colonel Alden's regiment mustered by Captain Lush at this lake Colonel Butler and Maor Whiting went to the foot of the lake to view that post.

June 23rd A number of boats provisions arrived at the lake this day.

June 24th Boats and provisions arrives at this lake very fast 500 waggons going steady—A soldier shot at the river this day for desertion.

June 25th A committee began to inspect the provisions at this lake found but little of the same damaged.

June 26th Colonel Duboise's regiment arrived at this lake and proceeded in boats to Lows Mills.

June 27th (Sunday) One of the Riflemen was fired upon by the Indians in Springfield, was wounded but made his escape with the loss of his fire arms.

June 28th Went to Camp Liberty at Lows Mills (and dined at that place) General Clinton gave each officer on the ground at this post one cag of rum containing two gall.—one man hanged at Mohawk River taken up for a spy from Butler's camp that's with the Indians.

June 29th The camp was alarmed by the firing some guns by officers going to Camp Liberty.

June 30th Nothing new this day.

July 1st 1779. Nothing new.

July 2nd General Clinton arrived at Lake Sago from Mohawk River, Colonel Butler's regiment and Colonel Gausewort's arrived and crossed the lake with the general and encampt at the foot of said lake, ColonelWisenfields regiment arrived at the lake but did not cross, the general ordered all the provisions to be moved immediately to the foot of the lake.

July 3rd Colonel Wisenfield's regiment and Colonel Duboise's crossed the lake and encampt with the other troops at that place, the general left Major Whiting with his regiment to bring up the rear of the army.

July 4th (Sunday) P. m. general and commissary general arrived at this lake with the rear of the stores, thirty Indians arrived at this lake to go the expidition with General Clinton, they were commanded by Colonel Hunyary.

July 5th The 6th Massachusetts Regiment crossed the lake with the rear of the stores and encampt with the rest of the troops at that place.

July 6th Rainy and very windy Colonel Rignier began to review the troops.

July 7th The 6th Massachusetts Regiment reviewed by Colonel Regnier.

July 8th Two of our centries fired on two men in the bush, supposed them to be spies—the officers drew each one cag more of rum.

July 9th. Pleasant weather.

July 10th Nothing new.

July 11th (Sunday) Heavy storm of rain.

July 12th Cool weather for the season.

July 13th Solomon Steel soldier in 6th Massachusetts Regiment dropped down dead as he was roling provisions to the store.

July 14th Alarm this night by the centries, firing some guns, supposed the saw men advancing to them but soon disappeared.

July 15th Took a tour on the lake fishing.

July 16th The weather cool for the season very unholesome at this place some days warm and the next after cool—a number of the troops sick with the dissentary.

July 17th Doctor Younglove arrived in camp from Mohawk River.

July 18th (Sunday) I attended publick service at this lake Mr. Greno delivered the sermon chaplain to General Clinton s Brigade, his text was taken from 22nd Job. 21.V.

July 19th Nothing new.

July 20th Major Dow arrived from Albany, (Captain Parker arrived from furlow in this camp) two deserters were brought to the 6th Massachusetts Regiment that had left it a few days agone, (Serjeant Spears and Johnathan Peirce.)

July 21st Three deserters brought into this camp (that had not left it many days) one belonging to the 4th Pennsylvania Regiment was tied up immediately and received 500 lashes it being back allowance due to him some days before he deserted and was forgave by his colonel.

July 22nd Began to build an oven for the regiment.

July 23rd An Indian arrived in this camp from Fort Schyler, informs that 1400 Indians and Tories were collected to intercept our march down the river.

July 24th Serjeant Spears whipped 100 lashes one soldier more 100 lashes with him—three men sentenced to be shot by the same general court martial Monday next.

July 25th (Sunday) Rainy weather.

July 26th The three prisoners reprieved until Wednesday next.

July 27th An express arrived in this camp this day informs, that General Wane has taken a small fort from the enemy at Stony Point on North River and captured 550 men—also informs that Major Hopkins with a number of officers from Colonel Warner's regiment are killed at Sabbath Day's Point, below Crown Point they were out on a party of pleasure, and were surprised by a number of Indians. Also informs that thirty two men and one lieutenant are killed and taken at the Areseo Fields near Fort Schyler, they were out making hay.

July 28th This morning 9 o'clock in Camp Lake Otsago Jonathan Peirce soldier in 6th Massachusetts Regiment Frederick Snyder 4th Pennsylvania Regiment Anthony Dunnavan 3rd New York Regiment were all brought on the grand parade to be shot to death for desertion the two former were reprieved and the latter shot to death—he deserted from Saint John s last winter and inlisted in Albany in ye 4th New York Regiment.

July 29th An express arrived this day informs that a body of the enemy has been discovered near Fort Schyler including some British troops.

July 30th Very pleasant weather which is something remarkable at this place.

July 31st Lieutenant Peebody arrived from Mohawk River with fat cattle for the use of the troops at this post.

August 1st Mr. Greno, delivered a sermon.

August 2nd Pleasant weather eat a rarity apples and cucumbers the first I have eat this year.

August 3rd Pleasant weather, an Indian arrived from Onida in this camp informs by a letter from Colonel Lewe that two Indians from the enemy brought in the account that 50 men had been killed lately at the Minisinks by Indians.

August 4th An express arrived from General Sullivan to General Clinton in this camp—informs that General Clinton's division will march in a few days.

August 5th Warm days and cool nights at this place.

August 6th Nothing new.

August 7th This day all the light infantry paraded, belonging to the several regiments was inspected by Colonel William Butler 4th Pennsylvania Regiment who is to have the command of them together with the Rifle corps.

August 8th (Sunday) All the boats loaded ready to proceed down the river tomorrow—this evening 6 o'clock the sluce way was broke up and the water filled the river immediately where a boat could pass, which was almost dry before—this lake is eight miles long and very level was raised in the upper part of it by this dike one foot perpendicular.

August. 9th The troops embarked on board the boats 9, o'clock this morning excepting those that went by land at 10 proceeded down Susquehannah River, 4th Pennsylvania Regiment in front 3rd New York in rear and arrived at Mr. Culley's Farm without much trouble by the crooks and turns in this river which are very plenty the land on the sides of this river very good and rich soil—Killed a large number of rattle snakes which were very plenty at this place, and very large came thirty miles by water and sixteen by land this day.

August 10th Rainy in the morning 2 o'clock p. m. embarked, and proceeded as far as Yokeum's Farm and encampt which is eight miles by water and five by land, the form of our march is as follows—Riflemen and light infantry in front commanded by Colonel William Butler, detached from each regiment to march opposite the boats with a strong rear guard cattle in centre.

August 11th Embarked 7 o'clock a. m. proceeded without much trouble as far as Ogden's Farm and encampt on the right of the river twenty-five miles by water and fifteen by land this day—the land very fine at this place, the land in general by the sides of this river when one side is good the other is barren—The general ordered each officer one quart of rum and one gill to each other man.

August 12th Embarked 7 o'clock a.m. arrived at the Scotch Settlement 2 o'clock p. m. Fifteen miles Ogdens where I went on shore and gathered a quantity of berrys and made a bowl of punch—Our troops burnt two houses, arrived at Unadilla 3 o'clock p. m. and encampt half a mile above Demini Johnston's Farm—the land very good at this place the houses are all destroyed by the Indians last summer—Some Indian tracks discovered by the front guard this day.—This is the place where General Hercamin held the first council with Brant and the Indians after this war commenced

August 13th Embarked 6 o'clock a. m. proceeded half a mile and halted by reason of the rapids proceeded on and encampt 4 o'clock p. m. on an Indian island which had ben improved by them left hand river twenty-five miles by water ten by land this day.

August 14th Embarked 9 o'clock a. m. proceeded on and arrived at Ocquaugo and encampt 5 o'clock p. m. the land very fine at this place ten miles by land fifteen by water this day—Some apple-trees at this place this is the Indian settlement that Colonel William Butler burnt last fall.

August 15th (Sunday) Mr. Greno delivered a sermon this day, a soldier of the 4th Pennsylvania Regiment died of a putrid fever and was buried under arms with three vollies fired over his grave. General Clinton is waiting for some militia to join him from the North River.

August 16th This Onnaquaugo is pleasantly situated on both sides of the river and on island in the centre the ruins of about sixty houses which appears by the cellars and wells that it was a fine settlement before it was destroyed considering they were Indians. One English family lived with them. 4th Pennsylvania Regiment went out to escort the militia into this place but returned without seeing them.

August 17th Fired a cannon this morning to inform the militia that the troops were not gone, embarked 10 o'clock a. m. proceeded on six miles and then made a halt to let the troops ford the river.—Burnt a number of Indians houses at the lower end of Onnaquaugo, some fine orchards with plenty of apples in them on the banks of this river, but the troops were not allowed to stop and get any of them—passed a large rapid and made a halt, this river is very crooked and you will run all points in the day—it divides in some places into six different streams—leaves one sufficient to carry a large boat.

Arrived at Tiscarora village about sunset and encamp right hand of the river—The Riflemen found some sides of tanned leather in a fat [*sic*] in the woods—made other discoveries found a dead man put under the roots of a wind fall (which was supposed him to be a prisoner that they had lately taken) found a war post which the Indians had put up with marks cut in the same in token of their scalps, and prisoners, destroyed two houses, discovered a *batteau* painted on a ledge of rocks left hand of the river which was a token that the Indians knew of their enemy's coming as the kept runners constantly before our army—came twenty-five miles by water and fifteen by land this day.

August 18th Embarked 7 o'clock a. m. proceeded one mile and burnt one house right hand of the river went a little further and burnt two more, arrived half a mile below Cheningo Creek and turned back to said creek and encampt the general detached a party of men to go up said creek and destroyed Cheningo town which was don—Two men from General Poor arrived to General Clinton and informs that General Poor will be within eight miles of this camp this night to escort General Clintons Troops to General Sullivan—came twenty-five miles by water and sixteen by land this day—Encampt right hand of the river.

August 19th Embarked 8 o'clock a. m. and proceeded on one mile and burnt seven houses, left hand of the river, went a few miles and burnt two more same side of the river. Arrived at Chukkanut, 9 o'clock a m. where General Poor's Division were encampt—About eleven hundred, men, burnt fivehouses at this place five miles by water and four by land from our last encampment to this place this is a fine large flat chiefly on the right hand of the river going down the army proceeded on and arrived at Owago about sunset this is a large Indian settlement and fine land—Encampt at this place, this is the Indian town that Serjeant Hunter was carried to that was taken 10th November last below Cherry Valley on this same river as he was returning with his scout—heavy rain this night, the general detached a party and sent them and burnt the town at this place about two miles up a little creek—eighteen miles by water and fourteen by land this day.

August 20th Heavy rain this day which detained the troops from marching—There was but one barrel of rum in the store which the general ordered to be equally divided between the officers which was one point each—The land which I have passed in general down this river is very good but when the flats are good on the one side the other is mountany and the flats narrow from the river.

August 21st Embarked 7 o'clock a. m. proceeded on our way and encampt 3 o'clock p. m. opposite an old Indian field about 500 acres cleared and very good—left hand of the river—saw some fine land on the sides of the river this day some pleasant mountains cleared by fire—discovered in the camp two Indian's bodies, lately buried only covered with turf, and the bones of one man that had ben burnt to death, saw the tree that they took the pitch splinters from, supposed him (that was burnt) to be an English prisoner they had taken, and this was done in revenge for one of their brothers that had been killed—Two of our boats ran on the rapids one of which was stove, both loaded with ordinance stores—fourteen boxes ruined 27,000 cartridges' in the same three barrels of powder we are now six miles from General Sullivan's camp—One Fitch Jerritt had lived at this place and is now with General Sullivan as a pilate—twenty miles by water fourteen by land this day.

August 22nd (Sunday) Embarked 7 o'clock a. m. Arrived at General

Hands detachment of light troops 9 o'clock a. m. where our troops were saluted from the land with thirteen cannon proceeded on one mile further and arrived at Tioga where General Sullivan's troops were campt on the west side of the river—Encampt half after 11 o'clock a. m. in an old Indian field a large quantity of land cleared at this place—which is very good the field officers all dined with General Sullivan this day—All mountains on the east side of this river at this place—Tioga Branch leads from this into the Cinnaku [Seneca?] nation—six miles by water and five by land this day.

August 23rd Captain Kimhal P. Master to Colonel Cilley's regiment this day was accidentally shot to death, and two soldiers wounded by the same gun that was carelessly discharged by a soldier, of said regiment—New Hampshire Forces—Fine pleasant weather.

August 24th Struck tents in the afternoon and proceeded on to our line of march. 6th Massachusetts Regiment joined General Poor's brigade.

August 25th The troops all ordered to march and leave the ground at 8 o'clock a. m. but were detained by a heavy rain.

August 26th 11 o'clock a. m. the army marched and left the ground proceeded on about five miles and encampt on a pine plain by the side of a large flat about 500 acres in the same well covered with grass—one deer ran through the camp.

August 27th Captain Day and Lieutenant Carter with twenty-five men from the 6th Massachusetts Regiment are left in Fort Sullivan with the baggage the army proceeded on this morning 8 o'clock over hills and mountains, made a halt for the pack horses and waggons to pass a large defile some men detached to get them over about sunset marched forward and arrived at a large Indian settlement 11.o'clock p.m. a large quantity of corn beans and other sauce at this place—the land very good, large flats—much trouble this day with the pack horses their loads often falling off.—came seven miles this day.

August 28th Pleasant weather—the troops lay on this ground until 3 o'clock p. m. waiting for General Clinton's Brigade to come on and to destroy the corn. After a signal of three cannon the army moved on the first for striking tents 2nd for loading the baggage 3rd for marching &c and proceeded over a large mountain about two miles high—arrived at Chemung about sunset and encampt near the river—came four miles this day.

August 29th (Sunday) This morning the camp was alarmed by the firing some guns, but turned out to be the Riflemen clearing out their arms—the army moved on. 8 o'clock a. m.—at 1 p. m. our front guard discovered the enemy's breastworks at Newtown—the army made a halt, and was ordered in line of battle—the artillery under the command of Colonel Procter soon began to cannonade their works with ball and shells—General Poor's Brigade were posted on their left and had to climb a large mountain while the savages kept a smart fire on them from the top of said mountain, but General Poor's Brigade soon gained the enemy's ground which were obliged to take to their heels for safety and leave a good deal of their baggage behind them—such as blankets, packs &c.—the enemy was soon attacked from right to left in one hour they left their works and fled before the brave continental troops leaving behind them, one of their chiefs and a number of others dead in the field—making in the whole fourteen Indians.

One Negro, and one white man, fell prisoner into our hands—their breastwork was made of pine logs covered with green skrub bushes that no one might discover the same until they were quite on it—it extended near half a mile in length and from their right to their left one mile and half—the loss of General Sullivan's army is one lieutenant three soldiers killed 34 wounded—including one major one captain—in the 6th Massachusetts Regiment one man killed six wounded included in the above number. Came five miles this day the name of the lieutenant that was killed was McColley—Encampt—large quantities of corn and sauce at this place.

August 30th The army employed this day in destroying the corn.

General Sullivan requested the troops to take half allowance for the present which was agreed to by the army as the corn and other sauce is very plenty at this place—the wounded with the waggons and part of the cannon, were sent down this night to Fort Sullivan.

August 31st 1779. The army moved on 11 o'clock, a. m. marched chiefly on plains and flats, had very fine marching this day—Encampt on a pine plain.

Our Riflemen discovered some Indians—twelve miles march to-day.

Sept. 1st The army moved on 10 o'clock a. m. marched five miles on this plain and came to a defile a large marsh on the left hand—The pack horses were detained some time by passing a narrow passage close under the mountain—soon arrived at a long-swamp, where the artillery and pack horses by reason of large gulley's and miry sloughs found it very difficult to pass—this swamp is nine miles through the army arrived at Queen Catherine's Castle 9 o'clock p. m. Excepting General Clintons Brigade campt in the swamp as it brought up the rear of the army could not get through—Some of the pack-horses died in this swamp and a number of them left with their drivers all night, as they could not reach through—the Indians had left this place but a few hours, when our front guard arrived, as their fires were burning—there was a creek ran through this town, there was five houses one side of said creek and six the other—the Queens Pallace was a gambril ruft house about thirty feet long and eighteen wide—I campt by the side of a log on a piece of bark that came off one of their houses, by a fire the Indians had left, without any blanket, as my baggage tarried all night in the swamp (I was very cold) the worst rout this day I have seen on the march—came fourteen miles this day.

Sept. 2nd This day the troops were employed in washing their cloathing (and lay still to recruit the horses) and let the rear of the army come up &c. the general detached a party of volunteers to pursue the enemy, but returned without discovering any of them—Our troops found an old Indian squaw at this place that the Indians had left by reason of her being so old that she could not travel with them—the land is very good at this place, owned all by this Queen—there was one Dutch family lived here, and are gone off with the rest; there was a number of feather beds found in his house and two horses found in his fields.

Sept. 3rd The army moved on at 8 o'clock a. m. marched in the Indian path, the roads very good this day—passed some fine land timbered with oak and walnut—marched by a creek, which ran through a large meadow—Our front guard discovered some Indians in a corn field, which fled and left their kettles on the fire—Encampt on a heighth about six miles from an Indian village—the horses had only bushes for forrage this night—came twelve miles this day.

Sept. 4th This morning the troops were ordered to march at sunrise, but were detained by reason of the rain—the Army moved on 9 o'clock a. m. arrived at an Indian settlement 11 o'clock a. m. where we burnt six houses and destroyed some fields of corn, joining the Cinnaka Lake—where I had a full view of said lake, and appeared to me like a small ocean—the land the army marched over this day, is very fine and not mountany—some of the pack-horses gave out and died under their loads partly for want of forrage—General Sullivan sent off two Indians as expresses one to Colonel Broadhead the other to Onida (those two Indians were from Onida). Encampt on a piece of fine land, little or no underbrush, wooded chiefly with white oak—the horses had bushes for fodder this night—I gathered a quantity of wild oranges this day as large as common limes—the enemy had wrote on several trees that General Sullivan might pursue, but would soon meet with trouble.

Sept. 5th (Sunday) The army moved on, 9 o'clock a. m. the land our army marched over this day is very good and level. Passed two large gulleys which made it very difficult for the pack horses to pass—the army arrived at Appletown or Saint Coy. 2 o'clock p. m. where we found thirteen houses and a large old orchard and some peach trees—Three grand tombs where it is supposed they buried some of their chiefs, they were all painted very fine, and covered with a frame and bark, on the top of the whole—some of the houses were made of hewed timber and one of them had a chimney in it. Eleven of those houses stood on a ridge about sixty rods long and twenty rods wide; on this place stood the orchard which appeared to be planted many years.

Near this town was all bushes the piece I have mentioned, only excepted, which is a custom with them to have no land cleared near their houses: their cornfields were about half a mile from the town but the corn was chiefly gone before the army arrived—The army encampt at this place—A prisoner came to our army informed General Sullivan that he left the Indians last Friday and made his escape—he was taken by them last summer at Wyoming and brought to this place—says that the enemy left this town last Thursday and Friday, and that their strength. Now with Butler is about seven hundred Indians and Tories and that Butler means to fight us again—the general or-dered' the apple trees all girdled or cut down which was done — the houses burnt—came six miles this day.

Sept 6th This morning the army was detained from marching, by reason of the guards losing sixty or seventy head of fat cattle last night—A party of men were sent out in quest of them, and found about half of them—the army marched on at 2 o'clock p.m. proceeded on about four miles and encampt near the lake which is at this place, about eight miles acrost the water very clear and gravelly bottom—came over fine land this day and level—came four miles this day.

125

Sept. 7th The army moved on at 8 o'clock a. m. proceeded on eight miles and came to the foot of the Great Cinnakee Lake about 12, o'clock a. m. the army forded the outlet of this lake which was two rods acrost about two feet deep the water, with a swift current—the army marched on the beach at the foot of this lake, from one side to the other, which was about three miles—Swamp on the right hand and water on the left, this lake is forty miles long and eight miles wide at the widest part—the land on the west side is very level, and not mountany—eighty miles from Tioga, to the foot of this lake.

The army burnt two houses at the foot of this lake, was said they belonged to the Cinnakee King and made use of one of them as a summer seat—the army proceeded on two miles and arrived at Cannondesago the Chief Cinnakee castle about dusk, where we found about eighty houses somthing large—some of them built with hewed timber and part with round timber and part with bark. Large quantities of corn and beans with all sorts of sauce, at this place a fine young orchard, which was soon all girdled by the pioneers—this town lays very compact not more than 100 rods from outside to outside, came ten miles this day—the foot of this lake lays exact east.

Sept. 8th This day the army lay at this place to recruit—The general sent a detachment to destroy some houses and corn, on the sides of this lake, which was done—at our first arrival at this place, there was found a man child about four years old naked, left by the savages. Must be the child of some white prisoner they had taken.

Sept. 9th The troops were ordered to march at 6 o'clock this morning, but were detained by reason of a heavy rain—Captain Reed set out for Fort Sullivan with the invalids from this place—The troops moved on 11 o'clock a. m. and marched the artillery in an Indian path—the Indian fields continued near five miles on our way from this castle, very good road this day—excepting one small swamp but passed the same without much trouble—After marching seven miles came to a brook, the first water the army passed this day—three brigades crossed the brook half a mile and encampt—General Clinton's brigade did not cross—came seven miles and half this day.

Sept. 10th The army moved on 8 o'clock a. m. proceeded on four and a half miles through swampy ground, and then arrived at an Indian field, which continued for some miles—Came to a large lake forded the outlet, which was two feet deep about, four rods acrost, proceeded half a mile and arrived at Cannonowago—a Ginnacee Castle where was nineteen houses about 1 o'clock p. m. fire was set to then soon which consumed them to ashes in a short time—the army proceeded on half a mile and encampt near their corn, which was in great plenty, near a mile in length. Came nine and half miles today.

Sept. 11th The army moved on 6 o'clock a. m. (as the corn was destroyed yesterday) had very good roads this day the land very good and leval passed a number of Indian fields which were all covered with large quantities of Indian grass—Arrived 3 o'clock p. m. to a Ginnacee Castle of eight houses. Great plenty of corn and beans at this place, the army encampt (this castle called Onnayayon) this town is on a fine piece of intervale land and well waterered by fine springs and a small brook running through the same, which is very rare to be found in this country and in general the towns I have passed stand on poor land.—Came thirteen miles this day.

Sept. 12th 1779 (*Sunday*) The troops were ordered to march this morning at 6 o'clock, but were detained by the rain, the army moved on 1 clock p. m. and proceeded four miles and came to a lake which was on our left hand, forded the outlet which was one rod acrost and one foot deep with water, (myself crosssed on a tree that was fell acrost the same) went seven and half miles further and the army encampt on the side of a large hill—where was but little or no underbrush—The general left part of the stores with one of the field pieces and a strong guard at the place the troops left this day—The rout very good this day—came eleven and half miles.

Sept. 13th The army moved on 6 o'clock a. m. proceeded on one and half miles and arrived at Yoxsaw, a Ginnasee town, where was ten houses that were soon burnt—great plenty of corn, and all sorts of sauce at this place. Great number of peach trees which our troops soon cut down.—The army made a halt at this place for breakfast and to distroy the corn—About 12 o'clock a. m. the Indians attacked a party of our men that were sent out yesterday as a discovering party commanded by Lieutenant Boyd, they were returning to camp and were about one mile from the same, when the Indians discovered them, with the lieutenant was a number of the Riflemen some musket men, and one Onida chief making in the whole 27 men.

Eleven of the number made their escape, the rest were killed and taken. Our troops were making a bridge acrost a miry river at this place (Whenden), our army moved on and arrived at, Costeroholly, (a Ginnacee castle) about sunset, where some of the enemy were dis-

127

covered but soon fled—Where was twelve houses which were soon burnt, by the men that escaped in the late action, we are informed that a number of the Indians were killed and that their number in said battle were 200—the Onida chief was killed and cut to pieces—came eight miles this day.

Sept. 14th I should mention that the Riflemen yesterday took 100 pack that the Indians had left in their flight—together with their kettles and blankets.—The army was employed this forenoon in distroying the corn at this place, which was done by throwing part of it into the river and part was burnt—The army moved on at 1. o'clock p. m. and forded a deep creek, crossed the large Ginnacee flats two miles—Forded the Ginnacee River eight rods acrost, and knee deep, swift current, which made it very difficult to pass—came on a height the other side of this flat, where I had a full view of the same and suppose there is 10,000 acres in it of cleared land level and all covered with grass as high as a man's head—proceeded on over hills and swamps and arrived sun one hour high at night;—at the grand Ginnacee Castle where was 120 houses the most of them compact together—where at our arrival we found the body of the brave Lieutenant Boyd and the body of one of the serjeants that was with him both of their heads cut off, the lieutenant was all skinned, his back much bruised, his nails burnt out, and many stabs in his body; his brother sufferer was in the like condition, with a knife sticking in his back—their bodies much eat by dogs—The army encampt at this place—came six miles this day.

Sept. 15th This morning the whole army was ordered out to distroy the corn at this place two thirds at work while one third guarded them;—this was done by carrying part into the houses, which were saved for that purpose, the biggest part was burnt in the fields, there was the largest quantity of corn, beans and all sorts of sauce at this castle that I have seen in one place on my march, as it was their head castle It was supposed by the army that there was 1000 acres at this place, and the land very fine and rich—The land from Yoxsaw to this appears to be the best in this country that I have seen though in general all very good, but not well watered.

A woman and little child came into our camp this day, that the enemy had left behind them, she informs General Sullivan, that she was taken from Wyoming by the Indians last summer, and had ben with them ever since; likewise informs that the enemy are much distressed with hunger and frighted at the approach of the general's army, and thinks he is bound for Niagara—1 o'clock p. m. the army left this place and began their march back for Tioga as they are now 150 miles from the same.—Set this town all in flames as there has not one house ben burnt since our arrival, but as I mentioned before were referred to distroy the corn in—Crossed the large river (I mentioned before) about sunset and encampt on this large flat near Casteroholly.

Sept. 16th This morning the army was employed in distroying corn that was left when the army moved up, which was in great plenty on this flat. The army moved on at 9 o'clock a. m. and arrived at Yoxsaw 3 o'clock p. m. where the army halted and encampt to distroy corn that was left at this place—Our dead was gathered together and buried, that was killed ye 13th instant, thirteen white men and one Indian was found dead in a small compass of ground, they were all scalpt and hakked with tommahawks, the Indian was cut almost all to pieces (it was Captain Hunyost from Onida) in the whole sixteen killed eleven escaped making 27 in the party—Hard frost this night.

Sept. 17th The army moved on this morning 6 o'clock and arrived at Onnayauyan—12 o'clock a. m. where we found our stores in good order, the troops that were left with them had made an abbertee [abatis?] fort for their security against the enemy.

Sept. 18th This morning the army moved on at 7 o'clock arrived at Cannonowago 4 o'clock p. m. forded the outlet of the lake and encampt—a number of Onida Indians with one of their chiefs met us this day.

Sept 19th Sunday The army moved on this morning 7 o'clock arrived at the Half Way Brook 12 o'clock a. m. and made a halt for the troops to refresh themselves three men as express from Newtown, met General Sullivan this day informs that there is six days' provisions for the army at that post proceeded on and arrived at Cannondesago, sun half an hour high at night, and encampt on our old camping ground.

Sept. 20th This forenoon the army lay at this place the general detached a party under the command of Colonel Gansewort to proceed for Albany after the baggage that was left at that place—another party up the side of the Cinnakee Lake to destroy corn—the army moved on 3 o'clock p. m. forded the outlet of the lake and marched about one mile and encampt.

Sept. 21st The general detached a party this morning commanded by Colonel Durbin to go to the other lake to burn some houses and distroy the corn &c. at that place—The army moved on this morning at 7 o'clock proceeded on and arrived at Appletown 2 o'clock p. m. proceeded on a few miles farther and encampt near the lake where had ben an old Indian settlement—4 o'clock p. m.

Sept. 22nd The army moved on this morning 8 o'clock proceeded on our march campt eight miles from Queen Catharine's Castle on a pine plain near a brook—a large buck ran through the camp this evening.

Sept. 23rd This morning the army moved on at 7 o'clock arrived at the Queens Castle 12 clock a. m. where the army made a halt found the same old Indian squaw that was left at this place when the army went up—the army proceeded on four miles and encampt in the long swamp.

Sept. 24th This morning the army moved on at 8 o'clock proceeded on and arrived at Newtown 4 o'clock p. m. where we found the stores under the command of Captain John Reed 6th Massachusetts Regiment The army was saluted from the fort with thirteen cannon which were returned from Colonel Proctor's artillery—the troops drew one gill of whiskey each man, and one pound and quarter of beef the first allowance the troops drew this month more than half a pound beef per day per man and *ditto* of flour—there has not been one storm to detain this army one day since they left Tioga which is thirty days.

Sept. 25th Those forks of the river at this place are called the one Tioga branch the other Keugah branch, both empty into Susquehannah River. The army lay at this place this day and the future joy [*feu de joie?*] was fired in this camp at 5 o'clock p. m. The general made a present of an ox to the officers of each brigade and likewise to the core of artillery—each officer half a point of rum and each other man one gill of whiskey.

Sept. 26th Sunday. This day Colonel Derbin arrived with his detachment from his command and brought two Indian squaws prisoners with him—he informs that he has burnt a number of houses and distroyed a large quantity of corn.

Sept. 27th Colonel Cortland was sent with a detachment up Tioga branch to distroy corn which was in great plenty up this river.

Sept. 28th This morning about 9 o'clock Colonel Butler arrived in this camp with his detachment that had ben on the Frontiers of Keugo [Cayuga?] Lake, informs that he has distroyed a large quantity of corn and burnt a number of Indian towns—The sick were sent off this day from this place to Tioga, part by water and part by land, the artillery and ordinant stores, were all sent in boats down the river to Tioga, excepting the cowhorn [cohorn?].

Sept. 29th The army moved this morning at 8 o'clock arrived at Chemung 12 o clock. a. m. where the troops made a short halt, and then moved on, arrived at the camping ground, where we found the first corn going up. Encampt 4 o'clock p. m. eight miles from Fort Sullivan.

Sept. 30th I would inform the reader that Fort Sullivan and Tioga is one place. The army moved on this morning at 8 o'clock passed the large defile which was 200 rods between the brink of the mountains and the river—The army arrived at Fort Sullivan 2 o'clock p. m. and was saluted with thirteen cannon from the fort—which was returned with thirteen from Colonel Proctor's artillery, the troops passed by the fort and marched on to their old camping ground; and encampt—The officers all dined in the fort on a dinner ordered by Colonel Shreefe who commanded said fort while the army were gone on the expidition—The officers drew half a pint of rum each, the other troops one gill of whiskey each—This day completes thirty-six days since the army left this grownd, and has not ben detained one day by storms or any other accident.

October 1st 1779. Pleasant weather this day.

October 2nd The general gave orders for the troops to march Monday next at 6 o'clock—Fort Sullivan to be evacuated tomorrow morning at 7 o'clock.

October 3rd Sunday. This day the troops were employed in distroying the fort and throwing the pickets into the river which was near on both sides of the fort.

October 4th This morning the army marched and left the ground at 9 o'clock for Wyoming—came over skrub land this day—Passed a defile on the brink of the river where was a narrow path on the steep side of a large mountain about 200 feet perpendicular which made it very dangerous to pass; and was a sollid rock three horses with their loads fell off and dashed to pieces in the river—Proceeded on and encampt on the point of the river—Some rain this day and very hard this night—Came twenty-five miles this day—Part of the troops came in the boats.

October 5th This morning 11 o'clock the troops all embarked on board the boats, excepting a number to drive the cattle, and take down the pack-horses Proceeded down the river and encampt seven miles below Wylucee the boats came on very well, this day passed some bad rapids—This river on the sides is very mountany and opposite on the other side some small flats—Some of these mountains 300 feet perpendicular—Came twenty-one miles this day.

October 6th This morning the troops moved on at 6 o'clock proceeded down this river and encampt west side of the same on a piece of land that was cleared by girdling the trees and was covered with English grass—Came thirty miles.

October 7th This morning the army moved on and arrived at Wyoming 12 o'clock a. m. and encampt on a pine plain—the troops drew half a pint of Whiskey each—This river is very mountany, on the sides of it and opposite these mountains on the other side, some small flats which are very rich and good land, those flats from Tioga to Wyoming have all ben improved and cleared by girdling, but the houses are all burnt by the Indians—This Wyoming is pleasantly situated on both sides of the river and the land near the same very good—Came fifteen miles, making in the whole 91 miles from Tigo to this place by water.

October 8th pleasant weather orders this day for the army to march Sunday next for Easton,

October 9th Commissary Woodman left this place for Albany.

October 10th (Sunday) The army marched and left the ground 3 o'clock p. m. for Easton—Came over a large mountain very rocky and some muddy sloughs, arrived at Bullocks-Farm at a long meadow 11 o'clock at night where the troops encampt—Came seven miles this day.

October 11th This morning the army moved on at 8 o'clock very bad roads this day—Crossed the School-kill River encampt about sunset on a pine hill.—Came fourteen miles this day—Enterered the Pennsylvania line.

October 12th This morning the army, moved on at 7 o'clock and came into the bad swamp 3 o'clock p. m. Met a number of waggons from Easton to help on with the baggage—Rained very hard this afternoon, got through the swamp 4 o'clock p. m., the rout very stony and muddy this day crossed the Lehi River. Encampt about dusk on a pine plain—Came sixteen miles this day.

October 13th This morning the army moved on at 7 o'clock proceeded on five miles and arrived at Larnards Tavern, where was forrage for the use of the army—proceeded on and arrived at Brinkers Mills 5 o'clock p. m. where the army encampt and drew provisions, as there is a continental store kept at this place—Came seven miles this day—This place is west side the Blue Mountains.

October 14th This morning the army moved on 10 o'clock and crossed the Blue Mountains at the wind gate—Encampt east side of the mountains—The Dilleware and Lehi Rivers runs through this mountain—large fields of buck wheat in this place, which the men and women thresh in the fields the land very poor in general only some valleys improved—Came seven miles this day.

October 15th This morning the troops marched at 6 o'clock, proceeded on and arrived at Easton 1 o'clock p. m.—The land the army came by this day is very poor, chiefly skrub oak plains—The army encampt on the bank of the Dilleware River—The officers of the 6th Massachusetts Regiment dined in town this day, that was prepared by Captain Ballard as he has ben here some days—This Easton is situated between two mountains, and lays on Dilleware and Lehi River opposite the Gersies, the houses are chiefly built with stone and lime some of them very elegant—Came twelve miles this day, which makes 63 miles from Wyoming to this town.

October 16th This day I went into the Gersies after some markee cordage—A very poor place and the land very stony.

October 17th Sunday. The 6th Massachusetts Regiment mustered this day by Mr Nehemiah Wade Mr. Master—the troops attended public service in the new church in this town, the sermon delivered by Mr. Evins chaplin to General Poor's Brigade.

October 18th This day the troops were ordered to be barracked in town, those that had no tents to cover them—Captain Daniel Lane this day was discharged from the Continental Army By General Sullivan at Easton.

October 19th This day I rode with Captain Reed and some more gentlemen of the army to Bethleham a town twelve miles from Easton inhabited by Moravians. Arrived there 12 o'clock a. m. and dined at the great tavern as there is but one in the town, which is kept by the whole place as all their stores are put in public stock—after dinner was piloted through the town by a squire, went to the nunnery where was many curiosities carried on by the nuns, this house is very large and many rooms in the same which are filled with women of all ages, not mixed, but every class by themselves, in short all sort of work ever done by a woman carried on in this place, went into their place of worship, where were many grand pictures amongst the rest a near emblem of the sufferings of our Saviour—went into their bed chamber where were as many beds as nuns in the house, as no two of them sleeps together they are exceeding neat and clean with everything that concerns them—their custom at night is to keep one of themselves as a centry at the door of their chamber, which is relieved every hour, so that they may discover any man coming near them, they see no man but every Sunday, excepting those strangers that go to see their curiosities, which is the time that they expose of the works that supports them.

From this I went to the brother's house, where are many things worth seeing, but not equal to the sisters, those brothers all live in one house, but don't work in the same—Went to see the smiths, tanners, cloathiers, and all sorts of trades, which are carried on in the easiest manner all by water—the water is carried through this town to every house, after this manner, it is taken out of a spring by three pumps, which never stop carried by water, conveyed through a brass pipe up a steep hill into a cistern then taken twenty feet into the air perpendicular and from that conveyed through small pipes to all parts of the town, and is drew from a brass cock that stands in the street in a pump—this town is very pleasantly situated on Lehi River the buildings very elegant all stone and lime. These people put all into a common stock and from that draws their subsistance—left this town about sunset. Arrived at Nazereth 7 o'clock this evening, where we tarried this night. Seven miles from Bethleham.

Oct. 20th This morning went through this town, to see the situation of it, which is very pleasant but is a new place settled but six years—

All stone houses, the water is carried through this town, in like manner as in the other only it comes naturally from a spring of a heighth without the help of pumps and is carried underground in large wooden pipes.

Left this town 10 o'clock a. m. Arrived at Easton 1 o'clock p. m. the land between this place and Bethleham is very poor and sandy, they raise chiefly buckwheat.

October 21 and 22nd Nothing new.

October 23rd This day General Poor's Brigade crossed Dilleware River 10 o'clock a. m. marched five miles in the Gersies and encampt in the woods—Captain Lane set off for New Winsor on North River.

October 24th Sunday. Pleasant weather.

October 25th This day I crossed the Lehi River and rode ten miles in Pennsylvania to Colonel Larrick's for horses for the regiment and returned to camp in the evening, the land in this rout is very stony and rough.

October 26th Rode into Greenig town with Major Whiting and Adjutant White, and Pay Master, Tucker arrived at the regiment with money for the same.

October 27th The army marched on this day and encampt in Oxford, about eight miles from the ground we left, there was wood and straw provided at this place for the army this place is in the Gersies.

October 28th The army moved on this morning at 7 o'clock, proceeded on and arrived at Hardwick and encampt, near the Log Goal—came fifteen miles.

October 29th The army moved on this morning at 7 o'clock and arrived at Sussex Court House in Newtown 12 o'clock a. m. in the Gersies yhirty-nine and half miles.

October 30th This day the army moved on and arrived at Charcole Town twelve miles from the Court House, and encampt.

October 31st Sunday. The army moved on this morning and arrived at Warrick in the afternoon in the State of New York and encampt—Came fifteen miles this day.

Nov. 1st The army moved on this morning and marched over Sterling Mountains a very rocky, bad rout this day—Arrived at Sterling town and encampt near the furnace, which is built at the mouth of a small lake the land very rocky and mountany at this place—Came ten miles this day.

Nov. 2nd The army moved on this morning, and arrived at Rammessau in the Clove—eighteen miles from Kings Ferry—this mountain is seventeen miles very rough rout, and difficult for waggons to pass—Encampt in the woods—Came eleven miles this day—Lord Sterling's division has left this two days and gone to Kings Ferry.

Nov. 3rd Blustering and cool some squalls of snow.

Nov. 4th Major Whiting and Captain Reed rode into the country for a party of pleasure.

Nov. 5th The major and Captain Reed returned to camp this afternoon, the officers baggage arrived from New Winsor with their portmanteaus—Orders to march tomorrow morning 8 o'clock for Pumpton in the Gersies.

Nov. 6th General Hand's brigade and the artillery marched this day for Pumpton—the other two brigades were detained for want of waggons—I rode into the country to see a satyr which was twenty-four inches high drest in coat jacket and trowsers resembled a small Negro, would handle the fire-lock very well and go through any manoever that his master bid him.

Nov. 7th Sunday, General Clinton's brigade marched this day for Pompton.

Nov. 8th General Poor's brigade marched this morning and arrived at Pumpton 3 o'clock p. m. and encampt in the woods, General Washington arrived at General Sullivan's quarters this afternoon, about two miles from this camp. Marched twelve miles this day.

Nov. 9th This day General Washington rode through this camp.

Nov. 10th This day the 6th Massachusetts Regiment and Rifle Corps were ordered to march tomorrow for Westpoint.

Nov. 11th Were detained for want of waggons.

Nov. 12th 6th Massachusetts Regiment marched from Pumpton and arrived at Rammepo in New York State.

Nov. 13th Marched from Rammepo this morning and arrived two miles from King's Ferry on the North River, and encampt—Came seventeen miles this day.

Nov. 14th Sunday, This morning crossed the North River—Arrived at Peekskill and encampt about dusk—Came seven miles this day.

Nov. 15th This morning the regiment marched on and crossed the river and arrived in Westpoint 2 o'clock p. m. and encampt in the bush one mile and half down the river—came eight miles.

Nov. 16th Some snow this night.

Nov. 17th Cold and blustering weather.

Nov. 18th This day the 6th Massachusetts Regiment marched and joined General Patterson's Brigade very cold and blustering.

Nov. 19th Pleasant weather.

Nov. 20th This day sent the horses into the country to be kept as there was no forrage on the Point.

Nov. 21st Sunday, Rainy weather this day—Major McKinster and Captain Bussey came to see me.

Nov. 22nd This day the 6th Massachusetts Regiment was mustered by Colonel Varrick Muster master General this is the fifth day that the troops have drew no bread on this Point as there was none.

Nov. 23rd Drew some bread this day—very cool weather at this place.

Nov. 24 and 25th Nothing new.

Nov. 26th A smart snow storm this day—and the men in the tents which made it very tedious.

Nov. 27th The snow blew very much, and made it as tedious as the storm which crept into our tents very fast.

Nov. 28th Sunday. Pleasant weather this day and warm.

Nov. 29th The paymaster arrived with the cloathing for the regiment.

Nov. 30th This day the chane that crossed the river was removed by hoisting the same whole between boats and was taken to the shore to be laid up for the winter.

December 1st Five men discharged this day from the 6th Massachusetts Regiment.

December 2nd A still snowstorm began this morning, which cleared off with a heavy rain—made it very tedious in campt.

December 3rd and 4th Nothing new.

December 5th Sunday A tedious snow storm and wind this day.

December 6th Lieutenant Carter Ensign Bagnal, Ensign Parker, set out for home, on farlow from Westpoint.

December 7th Captain Ballard left Westpoint on furlow—Captain Reed, Pay Master Tucker and Lieutenant Givins went to New Winsor.

December 8th Captain Reed pay master and Lieutenant Givins returned to camp.

December 9th Thanksgiving-day the troops drew one gill of rum.

December 10th Some rain this day.

December 11th Nothing new this day.

December 12th Sunday some snow and heavy rain this day at Westpoint.

December 13, 14, 15, 16, and 17th Nothing new.

December 18th A tedious snow storm with hard wind which made it very bad in tents.

December 19th (Sunday) Went to General Heath's and got my furlow.

December 20th Left Westpoint on furlow lodged at Mr. Huestins six miles from said point the weather very cold.

December 21st Breakfast at Fishkill—Dined at Esq Storms's lodged at Colonel Moorhouse's thirty miles this day.

December 22nd Lodged two miles from Lichfield came twenty-five miles this day.

December 23rd Proceeded on, the roads very bad this day, and not broke, lodged in Symsberry at Landlord Garret's, eighteen miles from Lichfield twenty miles this day.

December 24th This morning proceeded on arrived at Springfield 6 o'clock p. m.—Lodged at Landlord Ede's eleven miles from Springfield—forty-one miles this day the roads very good.

December 25th Proceeded on—Lodged this night at Landlord Taft's—six miles west from Worcester—thirty-two miles this day.

December 26th Sunday Proceeded on and lodged at Colonel Mackintoshes in Needham—Came forty-seven miles this day.

December 27th Proceeded on and arrived at Stoughton sunset, the weather has ben very cold and severe since I left camp—twelve miles this day.

December 28th Some snow this day.

December 29, 30 and 31st Nothing new this day.

January 1st 1780. Pleasant weather.

January 2nd (Sunday) very cold this day and a storm of snow this night.

January 3rd Some snow and blustering this day.[3]

---

3. The original journal is now owned by Mr. William Henry McKendry, of Ponkapoag, Massachusetts, of the Harvard Class of 1882. By him it was lent to our associate the Rev. Henry F. Jenks, of Canton, who has compared the proof with it, and has made the essential corrections in the text.—J. W.

The New Hampshire Brigade in the Sullivan Campaign

DELIVERED AT THE ANNUAL MEETING OF THE N. H. SOCIETY,
SONS OF THE AMERICAN REVOLUTION, JULY 12, 1910.

BY WILLIAM ELLIOTT. GRIFFIS, D.D., L. H. D

No one of the thirteen colonies exceeded New Hampshire in the number of men, proportionate to her population, which she put into the field during the Revolutionary War. Out of the total population of 82,000 she sent seventeen regiments into the national service. As the number of men enrolled in 1775 was but 16,710, she virtually called upon all her sons of military age to serve the cause of freedom.

On reading the king's proclamation forbidding the importation of munitions of war into the American colonies—which meant royal coercion and war—Sullivan and Langdon began hostilities December 13, 1774, before the men of any other colony, by seizing the powder at Fort William and Mary, in Portsmouth Harbour. This was the beginning. At the end of the war there were New Hampshire troops still in the Continental service. Besides this striking numerical superiority and early activities around Boston, New Hampshire was behind no other colony in sending her sons over a wide area of territory.

To say nothing of those in the service on sea, in both men-of-war and privateers. New Hampshire men fought in Canada, under Arnold and Montgomery, and it was Gen. John Sullivan who so skilfully conducted the retreat. For his signal services in overcoming all difficulties he received appointment as major general. We find soldiers from the Granite State in Virginia and possibly further south, while on the western frontier, Bennington, which was then in New York, was virtually New Hampshire's victory, for Stark held her commission. All this long and glorious record of New Hampshire is worth recalling.

WILLIAM ELLIOTT GRIFFIS

MAJOR GENERAL
JOHN SULLIVAN

Like gold it does not dim, but a little burnishing in memory keeps it in full splendour.

On the other hand, as compensation, New Hampshire was never, during the war, invaded by the foe. Her soil was untraversed by foreign enemies and her coast was virtually immune from naval aggression, while from her port went forth a succession of victorious men-of-war, under the thirteen-striped flag, the first of the colonies. Then, with stars added to its blue field, they sailed under the stars and stripes of the United States of America. New Hampshire, in its legislative hall at Concord, possesses a portrait in oil of Johannes de Graeff, the Dutch governor of the island of St. Eustatius in the West Indies, who, on November 16, 1776, after reading the Declaration of Independence, ordered the first salute fired in honour of the American flag.

Nevertheless, to my mind, the crowning glory, above the many honours, won by the soldiers of New Hampshire was in the great march of 1779 through the western wilderness, which virtually destroyed the Iroquois Confederacy, opening the path of civilization westward, and, by putting an end to the flank and rear attacks by savages on our settlements along the long frontier, made Yorktown possible.

This expedition, for which Washington detached one third of the Continental army, had been made necessary by the formidable incursions of the red men along the whole frontier, from New Hampshire to Virginia. A special force of five thousand regulars, all picked and veteran, was to leave their bases of supplies, and, passing beyond the confines of civilization, was to disappear in the forest, floating, cutting and marching their way through the wilderness to the Genesee Valley. The goal was not the British fort at Niagara, but the capital town of the Seneca Indians, who were the scourge of three states. Such an expedition, with its need of elaborate and costly preparation and its vast risks, was decided upon only after full discussion and vote of Congress, and by arrangement with Washington.

A mutual agreement between Congress and the commander- in-chief was then made, that during that year, 1779, or at least while this army of chastisement was abroad, no important military operations should be carried on by the main army; for, subtracting the four brigades and the artillery and riflemen sent into the wilderness, our great Fabius had not left over ten thousand effective regulars, against a British army of over thirty thousand.

When it comes to the literary proofs and the written records of the witnesses, we are abundantly supplied with a correct knowledge of the great march. Of the extant journals of officers, numbering nearly fifty, New Jersey and New Hampshire furnished seven each. New York six, Pennsylvania four and Massachusetts one. That of Col. Adam Hubley of Pennsylvania, both for text and drawings, and for what a critical scholar wishes most to know, as to topography, Indian life, the details of the campaign, etc., is perhaps the best of all; but certainly next to Hubley's for exact information, vividness of presentation, elegant style, literary exactness and general value, I should award the prizes to Lieut.-Col. Henry Dearborn of the Third, and Maj. Jeremiah Fogg of the Second New Hampshire Regiments. In general it was the ministers' sons in the army that were the superior penmen.

The New Hampshire Continental Brigade, according to the roster made by Hon. Charles P. Greenough of Boston, consisted of the first, second and third New Hampshire regiments (Continentals).

Enoch Poor was brigadier-general, Jeremiah Fogg *aide-de-camp*, Elihu Marshall brigade major, and Rev, Israel Evans the chaplain. The colonels in their order were Joseph Cilley of the First, Lieutenant-Colonel Reid of the Second, and Lieut.-Col. Henry Dearborn of the Third. In August, 1779, for the purpose of this single expedition, there were transferred to Poor's brigade Alden's Sixth Massachusetts Regiment, under Maj. Daniel Whiting, and the Second New York Regiment, under Philip Van Cortlandt. When orders came detailing the brigade for "the western expedition," they were in camp at Redding, Conn., where they had wintered.

Their first notable work was to be the arduous one of helping to build a road from Easton to Wyoming over the Pocono Plateau, now traversed by the Lackawanna Railroad. At Redding, Conn., they began to construct their winter huts, December 4, 1778. These they finished in a short time and tarried in them till the 10th of April, when they went to the highlands on the North River and stayed until May 9, 1779.

Two or three of the journals gave daily details of the march through New York and New Jersey to Easton. Ensign Daniel Gookin tells us that his regiment started from North Hampton, N. H., May 4, and after moving through the Massachusetts towns past Springfield, his dog Bark left him. Thence his route was through Connecticut to Salem, N.Y., to Fishkill, where he moved over the North River, lodging at Newburg, at which General Poor arrived to take command. The weather through New Jersey was very wet. Near Easton he was surprised at the fine mills built by the Moravians and, in the city, with the solidity of the stone dwellings and public buildings. He said he heard a sermon "in Dutch," which of course means German, and noticed the fine music of the organ. In the afternoon he went to church and heard a sermon preached by the chaplain of the New Jersey brigade. Each of the brigades had a spiritual adviser, who in every case was a man of ability and character who is remembered in history. One of these, the Rev. Israel Evans, who is commemorated by a bronze tablet on the walls of the First Congregational Church in this city, served during the whole Revolutionary War, first with New York regiments and then as chaplain of General Poor's New Hampshire brigade, acting for a time as *aide-de-camp* to Sullivan.

Some of the New Hampshire men made a pleasure ride up the Lehigh River to the bright, clean town of the Moravians, Bethlehem, which, during the whole war, remained the chief place of hospitals for the Continental sick and wounded.

At Easton, where the artillery was parked and the troops assembled, they were obliged to wait until June 18. Sullivan was harassed by the delays and lack of provisions and supplies, and most of the meat was spoiled before it could be used. The excuse given was that the coopers were all away with the Continental army, and the old casks being all requisitioned, only green timber could be used, which, in summer especially, soured the brine and ruined the contents. Writers like Bancroft, who have not appreciated the purpose, the difficulties or the value of this expedition, even as at the time people did not understand its large proportions and true object, have blamed Sullivan, when the fault was not his. Happily, however, as the optimistic Major Fogg afterwards wrote, these very delays actually furthered the success of the expedition. The time lost in waiting was utilized by unhurried nature to ripen the corn, pumpkins and other vegetable food for what the Continentals called "the Succotash Campaign," though the diet was occasionally varied with deer, turkey and rattlesnake meat.

Capt. Daniel Livermore of the Third New Hampshire Regiment gives the detail of the march from Newburg to New Windsor in New York, to Bethlehem, to Bloomsgrove Church, Chester to Warwick, to Hardistan and through New Jersey to Sussex state house, to Easton.

At Easton the troops were several times reviewed by General Sullivan and were exercised in the manoeuvres of forming and displaying columns, crossing defiles, etc. They left Easton with regret, finding it a pleasant town, and on Saturday, June 19, started northward to pass through Wind Gap, this being the only opening for many miles in the long chain of the Appalachian Mountains. Thence their march was to be over the desolate Pocono plain, two thousand feet high, now traversed by the Delaware, Lackawanna & Western Railway. Far-seeing Washington's purpose was, not only to destroy savagery, but to open the pathway of civilization westward, and Sullivan did it.

The road which he cut through the wilderness became afterward the pathway of the pioneers, who cut down the forests, built homes, seeded the new clearings and the old maize lands of the Iroquois, reared the church and schoolhouse and changed the wilderness into a garden. In the view of humanity this expedition was for the rescue of captives and the protection of homes on the border; in the eye of strategy, it was to ruin the enemy's granary, put to an end his flank and rear attacks, and prepare the way for Yorktown.

Let us pause here and take the point of view of a war correspondent on the ground, in the early summer of 1779.

The main army, making rendezvous at Easton, consisted of the Pennsylvania, New Jersey and New Hampshire brigades. Proctor's regiment of artillery, with nine guns, two being heavy howitzers throwing shell, one hundred and fifty fifers and drummers, three hundred and fifty riflemen, with pioneers and axemen, teamsters, surveyors and various assistants, numbering in all thirty-five hundred. The expedition is to have a total strength of probably six thousand men, of whom nearly five thousand are combatants. Seven hundred boats in all will be employed, and from Wyoming, one thousand, two hundred pack horses.

The wisdom of Washington is strikingly displayed at especially four points: First, in utilizing the waterways as far as possible; second, in insisting that the artillery, even the heavy guns, shall be taken along and carried as far as they may be floated on boats, leaving the lighter pieces to be drawn by horses and men to the goal of the expedition—the great Seneca town on the Genesee; third, in having every rod of the way measured by surveyors, for the great commander expects success and has an eye to the future; and lastly, in the selection of the personnel, on whom everything depended.

Except the splendid body of New Jersey veterans, the men were drawn from the three states with the longest of exposed frontiers,—New Hampshire, New York and Pennsylvania. Endless jeering was made and fun poked at the idea of taking artillery into the wilderness; but Washington knew the Indian as few of his soldiers did, and he was convinced of the demoralizing effect of cannon upon the savage.

Subsequent events fully justified his wisdom.

As to the commanding general, what we say on New Hampshire soil concerning him, to whom this great work and responsibility for five thousand men to be taken into the roadless forest country of a subtle enemy, we should say in every state of the Union or beyond sea. No better man could have been chosen. Sullivan was to be pitted against able foes, white and red. The Iroquois and Butler's Rangers from Canada were versed in all the lore of woodcraft. The march was to be for three hundred miles, much of the way through the twilight of dense woods.

There were no bases of supplies, no hope of a retrieval in case of defeat, no hospitals, no cities, towns or villages at hand. Every pound of flour and ounce of meat had to be carried on the backs of horses, while no provender could be carried for these patient brutes. They must subsist as best they could. Even the military evolutions must be performed, as it were, in the twilight of the all-encompassing foliage. Washington chose the right man for the work when he selected Sullivan, the New Hampshire leader.

Apart from being inured to the hardships of the frontier, New Hampshire men knew how to handle the axe. Accustomed to hard work in the open, and good marchers, no obstacles of swamp, morass, hill, defile or rocky steep could daunt them. Van Cortlandt's and Spencer's New York regiments had been detailed to open a road through the forests of Pocono Plateau, and on the 7th of May Colonel Cilley's First New Hampshire regiment, was sent to assist in the arduous work of laying corduroy in the swamps. By June 14 they emerged from the shades of the forest. The sight of the lovely Wyoming Valley must have seemed like a garden of the Lord—a Promised Land beckoning them to victory.

Four days later the main army, with the artillery and wagon trains, started from Easton, soon leaving behind the magazine of supplies, ever since called "Sullivan's Stores," and the last human habitation—a log cabin sixteen miles from Wind Gap, the gateway out of civilization. Over stony ground and quaking bog-covering of logs laid on mire and marshes, and through the gloomy swamp called "The Shades of Death," yet with occasional glorious mountain views of inspiring scenery, the terrible march of sixty-five miles was finished on June 23 at Wyoming.

We pass over disappointments, delays, and all things vexatious— only noting the cruelty of armchair critics and disparagers ignorant of the situation—and note that Sullivan, unappalled at the poor equipment and commissariat and the absence of promised reinforcements, gave the order to advance at 1 p. m. July 31, on the firing of a signal gun. With banners flying, drums beating, fifes screaming and Colonel Proctor's regimental band playing a lively air—probably the "*White Cockade*," or possibly "*Yankee Doodle*"—the whole army and fleet moved simultaneously forward, the entire force on land and water stretching out in two lines nearly a league.

Yet it was not all plain pushing, poling, sailing or marching. The boats must move upward against the current; and, between the difficulty of breasting the Susquehanna Rapids, surmounting the rifts and avoiding the shallows, and of getting on with packhorses not over-skilfully loaded and given to stumbling, falling and losing their packs, the dignity of the array could not be maintained by either boats or animals, up to the same standard exhibited by disciplined and intelligent human beings. Indeed, along the whole route there were many things to tickle the risibilities of the general and officers, and sometimes a sense of humour prevailed over the theories of discipline. Passing the fort, they received a salute of thirteen guns, which was answered by an equal number of "honour shots" from the fleet.

Naturally the marching men made more progress than the boats, for the latter were manned by crews not trained to their business. The down-rushing waters opposed the advancing scows, the channel was unknown, the current was swift and the shallows and risks were many. Above the boatmen, on the right and left, in the many gaps made by the great river, rose the cliffs, two or three hundred feet high. In many places the army had to climb the heights, following the great "Warrior Path." Over many a steep place tremendous difficulty was found in getting the heavily laden horses and the cattle forward. But day by day the men learned by experience in their new duties, though Cilley's regiment, on one occasion when on duty as rear guard, was all night long and until two hours after sunrise picking up the stragglers. The windings in the river made the distance for the boats greater than for the men.

Besides, there were various streams to be forded and all along were indications of lurking savages. Sullivan, taking no risk, and determined above all, whatever else would happen, not to be "Braddocked," doubled his flanking guards when he came to Wyalusing and elaborated a rough system of signals, so that information could be communicated to all parts of the army. Now began the casualties. A boatman fell overboard and was drowned. A New Jersey sergeant died suddenly, after marching all day. A cattle guardsman, temporarily left behind on account of sickness, was found dead. Each of these men was given an honourable burial. Despite the heavy rain, while the army rested, a New York sergeant with three men and a Stockbridge Indian were sent ahead as scouts and ordered to go as far as Tioga Point. Today along the line of the Lehigh Valley Railway, over and past places since made historic, the army pushed its way, passing Standing Stone, and moving over the precipitous ledge of rock, where, for more than four hundred feet, the path lies along the crest, two hundred feet above the level of the river.

It is no wonder that on that hot day of August 9 some of the men gave out and had to be carried in the boats, while three of the cattle fell off and were killed. Among the rifts and shallows the boatmen were wearied almost to death, so that the fleet fell behind the army. On the other side of the river the first applications of Washington's torch—that flame-kindler which gave his name ever afterwards among the Iroquois, of the Town Destroyer, was made when Captain Gifford burned the Indian town of twenty-eight new long houses.

At the ford of Sugar Creek the wary Sullivan, fearing a possible attack, reinforced Gifford with Cilley's and Van Cortlandt's regiments. Nothing happened, however, and at the present village of Milan, a mile below the junction of the Chemung and Susquehanna Rivers, the whole army forded the river, slinging their guns, powderhorns and cartridges over their shoulders. Holding each other by the hand, or linking arms, the men stepped in and waist-deep crossed through the swift current. After a mile's march they reached Tioga Point, where the whole army, including the right wing from Schenectady and the left from Pittsburg, were expected to join forces and then attempt the wilderness by striking northward through the lake country and westward to the Genesee.

Before these New Yorkers came, and on the same night of his arrival at Tioga, August 11, Sullivan, having sent out a scouting party, received word that the enemy were near. This determined him at once upon a night attack at 8 p. m. on the 12th. Taking most of the New Hampshire men and Hand's light troops, he plunged through the forest, over rocky ledges, tangled thickets, miry swamps and deadly defiles.

When near the Indian town which had been reported Sullivan sent Hand with his Pennsylvanians to strike the rear, while Poor and

GENERAL ENOCH POOR

ISRAEL EVANS
CHAPLAIN AND AIDE

his New Hampshire men of Cilley's First Regiment moved upon the front. Just before sunrise the two bodies of troops met, but the birds had flown. Having received word from their runners, the red men had utterly abandoned the place, so that nothing but the houses and hastily quitted debris were seen. The Pennsylvanians, eager to avenge Wyoming, pressed on with more zeal than caution and some of the New Hampshire men followed with them. While pursuing the Indians they came into a defile and ambuscade. From high ground they were fired upon and five men were killed and eight wounded, two being from Cilley's regiment.

With a cheer, our men rushed up the hill and sent the Indians flying in a moment; but crossing the river, the savages again stealthily crept near, fired a volley and wounded four or five New Hampshire men. Sullivan's orders recalled the soldiers, and wisely, too, from further pursuit. Sixty of the hundred or more acres of corn were cut down and the rest left standing for the future use of the army, on their return march in September. The troops, wearied with fatigue and the great heat, returned to camp, reaching Tioga on the 13th.

The seven corpses put on horses were brought to Tioga Point and buried, with solemn ceremonies, in one grave, Proctor's band playing the dirge, Roslin Castle, and the chaplain. Rev. Dr. William Rogers of the Pennsylvania brigade, officiating with a few appropriate words. The fourteen wounded were found rough accommodation in the log hospital.

Somewhat over a hundred years later, in digging for the foundations of the Tioga Historical Society building, wherein may be found a large collection of Sullivan data and relics from the Newtown battlefield, these bones, known from the records and recognized by their Continental buttons, were thrown out and honourably reinterred. Several of the men, who then or later died at this place were sons of New Hampshire and should be commemorated.

Meanwhile Sullivan was getting anxious about his right wing, consisting of the New York Brigade (which included the Fourth, Fifth and Sixth New York regiments); Alden's Sixth Massachusetts, Butler's Fourth Pennsylvania, Parr's riflemen and Lamb's artillery (two guns); in all about one thousand, eight hundred men and two hundred and fifty boats, under General Clinton, to whom he had sent orders to march and join him. Fearing that he might have been checked by Brant's movements, Sullivan determined to send a supporting column to meet him.

It is undeniable that Sullivan favoured the New Hampshire brigade, made up of men from his own state, but in a manner not to be found fault with. The favor which he showed them meant always hard work, with fatigue and danger. Having given Cilley's men an opportunity to show their mettle in pioneer road-making and in the first aggressive movement, he now selected about five hundred New Hampshire soldiers and joining these with an equal number from the Pennsylvania Brigade, on the 16th of August sent Poor and Hand with picked men northeastwardly to meet Clinton. Happily they had not to go very far. Clinton had started on August 9 and Poor's advance messengers reached him on the 18th.

The distance of the two corps apart was only nine miles, and General Poor heard with agreeable surprise Clinton's evening gun, which answered with a blast from the little coehorn mortar. The next morning, at a place, now on the Erie Railway, which took its name from the event, the two columns made Union. The united body, Clinton's brigade leading and the flotilla of boats (250) and Poor's reinforcements following, they reached Owego, and on Sunday, August 22, the whole force, on land and water, made a brilliant display, with flags flying and artillery booming welcome, the main army saluting with ringing cheers. On the way down Clinton's men had devastated the Indian villages and cornfields.

Let us now glance at the activities of the left wing, whose place of gathering was four hundred miles from that of the right at Schenectady. This left wing, under Colonel Brodhead, had started from Pittsburg on the 11th of August with six hundred and fifty men, with one month's provisions loaded on boats and packhorses, destroying, as they advanced, many Indian towns.

Sullivan received news by two runners, who reached him at Tioga Point, but Brodhead's men, getting as far as Hornellsville, were obliged to return for want of provisions, though not until they had wasted much of the Seneca country and decidedly weakened the enemy by drawing off five hundred warriors—at least one fourth of the whole fighting strength of the Indian Confederacy. In rags and barefoot and their pay nine months in arrears, and no money and no paymasters at Fort Pitt, these brave fellows continued patriotic and in service.

In camp, at Tioga Point, tents were cut up to make bags for the flour and these loaded on the horses and everything made ready. The whole army started on the 26th day of August up the Chemung Valley—men, boats, horses and cattle.

Sullivan had, from the first, determined not to be "Braddocked." Starting from Tioga Point up the Chemung River, amid mountains on every side and which sometimes came clear to the water's edge, where it seemed impossible to take an army and especially to move heavy guns, two days were consumed on the marches and fordings. He knew that from every hilltop savage scouts and Butler's rangers were watching his movements. With unsleeping vigilance he kept his riflemen ahead and on the flanks. His alertness was well rewarded. On Sunday morning, August 29, Parr's riflemen, being in the advance, seeing signs of Indians, a scout was ordered to climb the highest tree he could find and report.

A party of Indians had appeared ahead of them and, after firing their guns, had run off, expecting that these "Bostonians" would follow the example of most militia men, who, in pursuit, so often got into ambuscades. Parr's riflemen, of Morgan's regiment, however, were trained Indian fighters and used to stratagem. Instead of pursuit they waited for the report of the watcher in the treetop, who, after long scrutiny discerned Indians in their war paint beyond Baldwin's Creek. Peering longer and further, he discerned a long line of green running up the hill and most suspiciously regular. He was confirmed in his idea that here was art and not nature, when he noticed lines of young trees in the open space (where he knew had been an Indian village, named Newtown) that were set with a regularity unknown to nature.

Major Parr reporting to General Sullivan, the general commanding at once made his plans. Keeping back the cattle and horses under a guard, he ordered the riflemen to lie hidden along the banks of the creek to keep the enemy busy and be useful whenever an arm, head or leg showed itself. On the little rising ground, where today stands the Methodist meeting house at Lohman, Proctor's artillery was handsomely set in battery. Back of the riflemen, under cover of the cannon in the tall grass, Sullivan ordered the Pennsylvania light troops to lie down. He sent Maxwell's New Jersey Brigade out to the left, near the river, and in the defile, to be ready to act at the right moment. To Poor's New Hampshire Brigade he assigned the task of a flank attack on the right. The men were to go up along Baldwin's Creek about a mile and a half, climb the hill, reach the crest and then charge into the rear of the entrenchments. Clinton's New Yorkers were to follow and act as supports.

Now in an unsurveyed wilderness no commander can expect his subordinates to fulfil his expectation in point of time, especially when

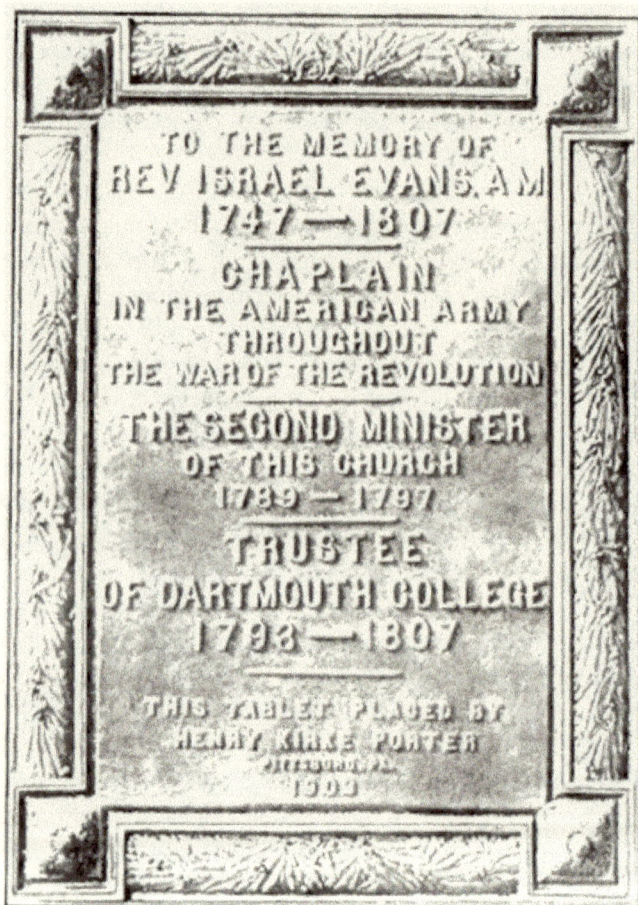

TO THE MEMORY OF
REV. ISRAEL EVANS, A.M.
1747 — 1807
CHAPLAIN
IN THE AMERICAN ARMY
THROUGHOUT
THE WAR OF THE REVOLUTION

THE SECOND MINISTER
OF THIS CHURCH
1789 — 1797

TRUSTEE
OF DARTMOUTH COLLEGE
1793 — 1807

THIS TABLET PLACED BY
HENRY KIRKE PORTER
PITTSBURG, PA.
1903

BRONZE TABLET ON THE WALL OF THE FIRST CONGREGATION-
AL CHURCH. CONCORD, IN MEMORY OF REV. ISRAEL EVANS.
PRESENTED BY HON. HENRY K. PORTER. PITTSBURG, PA.

the general supposes the utterly unknown ground is to be ordinarily level, instead of being a morass. After marching over a mile, floundering through bog and mire, wading through Baldwin's Creek, it took some minutes for the regiments to re-form. Then began the climbing of that hill, which, if one attempts the task on a sultry day in late August he can appreciate what the New Hampshire men had to do—especially when it was, in 1779, overgrown with scrub oak and tall trees.

Down below, Sullivan, not hearing the expected musketry fire on his right, so long waited for, three o'clock having come, and all the other troops in position, ordered Proctor to open with all his guns. Out flew the round shot from the five-inch howitzers and six-pounders, knocking out and ripping up the logs in the line of fortification and making great gaps visible. Then followed the grape from the smaller guns, while the howitzers and coehorn threw shell. The bombs, falling over and behind the Indians, were more terrible in their moral effect than if exploded among them. Soon it became impossible longer for Brant to hold his tribesmen, especially as the riflemen and light troops had begun to utilize the breaches in the fortifications to pour in a deadly hail of bullets.

By this time, at the extreme right, the Indian watchers on the hill-tops caught the gleam of bayonets and realizing the nearness of Poor's First New Hampshire Regiment, sent word to Brant, who rather welcomed the news. Leading off the main body of his savages from being targets for artillery into more congenial activities, this able chief prepared to envelop and destroy the Second New Hampshire Regiment, under Colonel Reid. In the movement Poor, with the First Regiment, was far away on the right, while Dearborn, on the extreme left, had hardly formed his men, so that Reid's Second Regiment was isolated and soon was enveloped by a semi-circle of red men yelling until hell seemed let loose, and firing as if they expected a quick harvest of scalps.

Happily Sullivan had ordered to go with each regiment a company of fifty of Parr's riflemen. It is my belief, though I may be wrong, that the New Hampshire men actually went into battle without their guns loaded. Some days before a messenger from Washington had reached the camp, bringing the news that Gen. Anthony Wayne, with his Pennsylvanians (after killing all the dogs in the whole region so that they could not bark) had actually taken Stony Point, without firing a shot, by the cold steel alone.

Now it would never do for men from the Granite State to believe, or have it even supposed, that Pennsylvanians—at that time Germans, Dutch, Irish and Scotch being in the majority—could ever beat New Hampshire men. Certainly the soldiers of Poor's brigade expected to repeat and excel Stony Point. They fixed bayonets before they climbed the hill. It was on record that not one of them at first fired a shot; but the riflemen, who had no bayonets, never let their guns be unloaded for a moment. They occupied the enemy with a smart fire until Reid's men could load; but for several minutes it looked pretty black, while a dozen or more of the Continentals lay dead or wounded on the ground. As matter of fact, most of the Americans killed or wounded in this decisive battle were New Hampshire men of Reid's regiment.

It may be safely said that Dearborn and the Third New Hampshire Regiment saved the day. Too far away from his commander. Poor, who was probably a mile distant, to get orders, Dearborn was yet near enough to Reid's regiment to see what the trouble was and to take in the situation. So, of his own initiative, he ordered his entire regiment "about face." Then, charging upon the Indians, he struck them in the rear. By that time Reid's men, covered by the riflemen, had loaded and seeing the help coming to them fired and then charged with the bayonet on the great body of Indians, first starting them on the run and then driving from tree to tree and cover to cover any of them who tried to make a stand.

Meanwhile, down below, Butler's Rangers, seeing inevitable destruction before them, began to retreat, some dashing across the river to save themselves. The moment Sullivan saw signs of wavering he ordered the Pennsylvania Light Troops to charge across Baldwin's Creek and over the entrenchments. Inside and beyond the lines there ensued a running fight with such brave Rangers or Indians who tried even for a moment to fire before their flight. As Maxwell's, Hand's, Poor's and Clinton's brigades, soon in sight of each other, realized their victory the whole host gave three ringing cheers.

Although only twelve corpses and two prisoners were found on the battlefield—for the wounded had been quickly conveyed away in canoes up the river—the signs of the dreadful work done by the shot and the shell of the artillery, to say nothing of the rifles and musketry, were abundantly manifest on the reddened grass, the torn and splintered trees, and the blood-bespattered packs and baggage. It is my own opinion that at least one hundred of that mixed host fighting for King George—Iroquois, Canadian Rangers, British Regulars, Tories and a few negroes, were put *hors du combat.*

The losses on our side were three killed on the field, Corporal Hunter and two privates, and thirty-three wounded, all but four of these latter being from Reid's Second New Hampshire Regiment. Among these were Maj. Benjamin Titcomb of Dover, N. H.; and Elijah Clayes, captain of the second company, both of the Second New Hampshire Regiment; Sergeant Lane and Sergeant Oliver Thurston; beside Nathaniel Macaulay of Litchfield, N. H., who died after an amputation, that night; while Abner Dearborn, a lad of eighteen and nephew of Colonel Dearborn, breathed his last a few days after in the rude hospital at Tioga Point.

Sergeant Demeret, Josiah Mitchell and Sylvester Wilkins died before September 19, thus making a total of eight men, all from New Hampshire, who gave their lives in one of the most significant, important and decisive battles of the whole war. Those who died upon the field were buried in different places, each one near the spot where he fell. To conceal the fresh broken earth of the graves and prevent desecration of the remains, fires were built over them. From Tioga Point such of the wounded as could endure the journey were sent by boat in care of Doctor Kimball, down the river to Wyoming, which place they reached September 2.

One may reasonably ask why, with apparently so much firing by such large numbers, the casualties were so few, yet it must be remembered that on our side, both the riflemen and the Pennsylvania Brigade, invisible to the enemy, were well protected by the banks of Baldwin's Creek on their front, and the enemy had no artillery; while in the real battle, on the upper heights to the right, our men had to charge up a steep incline, the savages probably firing over their heads. Down below the artillery did the main execution, both in taking life and by hastening demoralization, which in war is almost as important in effects as is carnage; indeed, it is often more. There was relatively also not a great use of musketry, for the only full regiments that actually faced a visible foe in force were the Second and Third New Hampshire. Then again, in the running fight through the woods, anything like a general slaughter was impossible.

On the British side, by their own statements, it was said: "Colonel Butler and all his people were surrounded and very near taken prisoners. The colonel lost four rangers killed, two taken prisoners and seven wounded," besides losing his commission, private baggage and money. The Indian record was found at the place called Catherine's

Town, four days afterwards, where a tree, marked 1779, and signed with Brant's name, had a rude picture of twelve men, each with an arrow pierced through his body, signifying the number of his men killed in the action of the 29th.

No wounded were found on the battlefield. As we all know, it was Indian custom to withdraw instantly the wounded and often the dead. This was done usually by attaching a "tumpline" to limb or trunk and drawing off the body; so that the curious sight of seeing an apparent corpse, or utterly disabled man, moving over the leaves and out of sight was often witnessed by the backwoods fighters in colonial and Revolutionary days. Each savage, before setting out on a raid, took an oath that he would perform this office for his fellow tribesman. It is known that several canoesful of wounded were carried up the river.

As late as 1903, Col. Ernest Cruikshank, in his *Story of Butler's Rangers*, admits a loss of five white men killed or missing and three wounded and an Indian loss of five killed and nine wounded.

It is not necessary to detail further the story of this expedition. Indeed, for dramatic purposes, to set the event most effectively in historical perspective after one hundred and thirty-one years, we might profitably stop at this point. Here was one of the most decisive battles fought during the whole Revolutionary War, for neither numbers nor area are necessary to effect enduring results. The truth is that the tribes of the Long House had gathered for a supreme effort and that the result was a virtual destruction of the Iroquois Confederacy. Furthermore, it ended the flank attacks on the Continental army and destroyed the dearly cherished hope of the British government to create in central New York a granary for the feeding of its armies.

To a great extent it weakened even the petty raids of the scalping parties, for the country was so absolutely devastated, that the Indians could not occupy the land either that season or, profitably, for several years. In the coming winter, too cold even for hunting, the discouraged horde huddled around Fort Niagara and were kept from starvation by salted provisions, imported mostly from Ireland. The Indians died like sheep in a blizzard. It is true that the very next year Brant led a large body of warriors as far as Tioga Point, but we never hear of their accomplishing anything important, while the injury done in the Mohawk Valley was very largely the work of Butler's Rangers, white men from Canada reinforced by British troops. This battle at Newtown on August 29, 1779. paralyzed the Indian Confederacy, so that it never was again what it had been since the advent of white men upon the continent, *viz.*, a powerful factor in international politics and war.

In a word, Sullivan carried out his orders given by Washington. He achieved the devastation of the Iroquois country. Striking northward, along Seneca Lake, to where Geneva now stands, he pushed forward to his goal—the great Seneca town in the Genesee Valley. Leaving the weak and lame at Honeoye, with a garrison and two field pieces, he made a forced march with two thousand, five hundred men, and at the outlet of Conesus Lake found Brant and Butler with reinforcements from Canada. These were all nicely hidden on the bluffs in ravines and at points of vantage, expecting this time, to a certainty, to "Braddock" Sullivan. The episode of Boyd's scouting party disturbed the nice calculations of Indian and Tory, for, fearing, as at Newtown, the flanking tactics of the New Hampshire men, the enemy broke his formations and fled. This was on the 12th of September.

The next day was given to destroying the great town of one hundred and twenty-eight houses, with the cornfields, which stood about where Cuylerville is today. The produce of two hundred acres of corn in ear and the gardens was levelled or cut down, piled in the houses and given to the flames. Several days were occupied in this work. Then the word, given September 15 at 2 p. m., was the joyful one of return. At Geneva, September 20, Sullivan sent Colonel Gansevoort home by the way of the Mohawk Valley. Col. William Butler, with the Fourth Pennsylvania, was ordered to move down the east side and Colonel Dearborn, with the Third New Hampshire, down the west side of Cayuga Lake. All were kept busy for many days in the common work of the main army, in desolating with sword and fire the Indian villages, forty of which in all, during the campaign, were given to the flames.

It was this devastation, peremptorily ordered by Washington, that gave him in Iroquois tradition the permanent name of "Town Destroyer." In this work Dearborn's troops occupied from September 21st to the 26th. Among places passed through and later the site of towns was Ithaca. Of the Indian villages burned, the most famous was Coreorganel, near the future University City. Thence across the country to Camp Reid, near the later site of Elmira and "four miles from where we fought the enemy the 29th of August," as Dearborn records, he joined the main body. The army had "a day of rejoicing" the day before, "in consequence of news from Spain,"—that is, recognition of the United States as an independent nation.

The return march, the destruction of Fort Sullivan at Tioga Point, the boat voyage down the Susquehanna, the traversing of Pocono Plateau and the arrival at Easton on the 15th of October followed in due course. On the 17th a solemn service of thanksgiving, with "A Discourse Delivered to the Officers and Soldiers of the Western Army . . . . by Chaplain Israel Evans to General Poor's Brigade" (and later printed in pamphlet form by Thomas Bradford in Philadelphia) officially concluded "the Expedition against the Five Nations of Hostile Indians," in which the men of New Hampshire made a vital factor.

In view of the historic facts, is it not the binding duty of the people of New Hampshire to rear on the Newtown battlefield some durable token of their appreciation of the services of their brave Continentals, who bore themselves so nobly in one of the most decisive battles of the American Revolution?

Sullivan's Campaign in Western New York 1779

By Simon L. Adler.

Read before the Rochester Historical Society January 14, 1898.

On the last day of July, 1779, after many and vexatious delays, General Sullivan got his army in motion and began his northward march for the country of the Iroquois. He had reached Wyoming on the 23rd of June with the main part of his force and had expected to find awaiting him there a complete supply of provisions and facilities for their transportation. But the quartermaster's and the commissary's departments had failed him and of the small quantity of provisions which had been forwarded very little was fit for use. Vigorous steps were at once taken to collect what was necessary for the support of the army; but even with the greatest efforts it was not until July 30th that the army was in condition for an advance.

Sullivan's orders were brief, but explicit. 'The Immediate object," said Washington, 'Is the total destruction and devastation of the settlements of the Six Nations and the capture of as many persons as possible.' The reason for this vigorous policy was later given by him in a letter to General Sullivan in which he emphasized the 'necessity of pushing the Indians to the greatest practicable distance from their own settlements and our frontiers; to the throwing them wholly on the British enemy,' and 'making the destruction of their settlements so final and complete as to put it out of their power to derive the smallest succour from them in case they should attempt to return this season.'

However we may judge the wisdom of this policy, in the light of subsequent events, it was demanded by the urgent appeals of the distressed population of our frontier settlements. From them came almost daily to the commander-in-chief and to congress tales of massacre and devastation attended with all the horrible details of Indian warfare. The massacres at Wyoming and Cherry Valley which even today, (at time of first publication), present to our minds pictures of murder and rapine, had just taken place. Every settlement on the long frontier line which protected the more populous districts of the young colonies, was in hourly fear of the tomahawk and torch of the Indian and of the equally bloodthirsty vengeance of the Tory.

The influence brought to bear upon congress, and the importance of preventing, and if possible shutting off forever, attack from this quarter is evidenced by the effective and for those days, large army placed under Sullivan's command. The men were well fitted, and the officers well selected for the work they had to do. Colonel Butler, probably the most able and active of the Tory leaders, said of them, 'Some of the best continental troops commanded by the most active rebel generals and not a regiment of militia among the whole.' Besides these disciplined troops, among whom were four companies of Morgan's celebrated Rifle Corps, nearly, if not quite as skilled in woodcraft as the Indians themselves, there were the pioneers of the Wyoming Valley inspired with the hatred which men feel whose homes have been burned, and whose kin have been murdered by the Indian foe.

Finally there were a few friendly Indians, principally Oneidas, to act as guides and scouts and to pilot the army through the dense and practically unknown wilderness. Not less fitted for the enterprise were the officers. General Sullivan had the confidence of Washington which had been won by the courage and skill he had shown in every position he had occupied; and the wisdom of his choice for the command of this important enterprise was justified by his careful and thorough conduct of the expedition.

General James Clinton, with the New York regiments, joined Sullivan on August 22nd. He had built a dam at the outlet of Otsego Lake, whose sparkling water and charming mountain scenery have been celebrated by the pen of James Fenimore Cooper, and on cutting it away was enabled to float his division well on the way towards its junction with the main army. Clinton had shown first rate ability in the French and Indian war and in the earlier years of the Revolution.

His experience on the frontier and his education as an engineer and surveyor well fitted him for an important command. The other brigadier-generals were Maxwell, Poor and Hand, all of whom had distinguished themselves in the war as capable and reliable officers. Hand, who was the youngest, had some knowledge of the Indian country and was familiar with their modes of warfare. His division had the right of the line and his movements were conducted with sagacity and spirit.

The route of the army lay northward along the Indian trail leading into the heart of the settlements and hunting grounds of the Iroquois. This pathway was narrow and inadequate for the passage of an army, but to stray from it meant to be lost in the wilds of an untraveled and unknown land. The Indian trails, worn deep into the soil by the tread of Iroquois *moccasins*, which had travelled for centuries these highways of the forest, were direct and clearly marked. On account of the skill with which they took advantage of the natural conformation of the land, and passed on their way the choice sites which have since been utilized for our cities and villages, these Indian paths were broadened into the highways over which the pioneers' wagon and the stage coach carried civilization into the wilderness of Central and Western New York.

The journals of the officers of the expedition, because of the difficulties under which they were written and perhaps in most cases of the practical temper of the men who wrote them, are meagre in detail, and are not inclined to abound in description of the country through which the army passed. Hardly had the march begun before it was in the midst of the beauties of the Valley of the Susquehanna. Lieutenant-Colonel Hubley, wrote in his diary on August 1st;

> To attempt a description of the most beautiful cataract at Lackawanna, called the Spring Falls, would be almost presumption.'

And on August 5th Dr. Jabez Campbell wrote,

> This place is a plain covered with English grass of an extraordinary growth and beautiful. In the way we passed a very high mountain, from which we had an extensive prospect of mountains and the river, a most beautiful variety.

The beautiful scenery called forth from time to time expressions of wonder and delight, despite the difficulties experienced by the army in making its way through this wild country. 'Through this country,' complains one officer, 'there is nothing but woods and mountains and swamps perpetually.'

Despite these obstructions the army made tolerable progress. The Indians closely watched it on its way but remained themselves unseen.

An occasional rifle shot, or the arrival within the lines of a back-woodsman who had barely escaped death and scalping alone told of their proximity. On August 12th, they appeared in some force near the present village of Chemung and firing on General Hand's brigade at short range killed six men and wounded twelve. They were immediately charged and disappeared in the forest. From this time the army proceeded with much greater caution and it was this alone that prevented an ambuscade which might have checked the expedition at Newtown, near the site of Elmira. Here the decisive battle of the expedition was fought. The British and Indians had carefully chosen their ground and masked their position with shrub oaks, cut the night before. The position was well selected and the enemy determined; and had the army marched blindly along the trail it probably would have been cut to pieces.

But by means of climbing tall trees and surveying the path for a considerable distance ahead, the riflemen in advance discovered the works of the enemy in time. General Sullivan called a council of his officers and a plan to dislodge the Indian and Tory forces was agreed upon. Its wisdom was justified by its complete success. Every effort of the Indians to draw the American forces in front to an attack, before the flanking divisions which had been sent out to the right and left had attained their positions, failed.

When all was in readiness the cannon which had been advantageously placed began to play upon the enemy's works and the advance was begun. The Indians fought with a remarkable steadiness and bravery, when we remember that the roar of cannon and the bursting of shells is most terrifying to Indian ears. When they found that they were practically surrounded they began a masterly retreat about seven hours after the first gun was fired; and succeeded in carrying off the greater part of their killed and wounded.

The American loss, three killed and thirty-nine wounded, was remarkably small considering the number of men engaged, and the length of the battle. It has been impossible to ascertain the British and Indian loss, but it must have been much greater. There have been various estimates made of the numbers engaged on either side. The British say that they had in the fight from four to six hundred Indians and two hundred English, which probably is fewer than there were; while Sullivan's estimate of their numbers at fifteen hundred is undoubtedly too great.

This estimate is made from the number of men it would take to man their works. To have properly defended the long line which they occupied would need many more men than they had so that they concentrated their force at certain points in the line, leaving the intervening spaces barely protected. The number of Americans engaged seems also to be uncertain, but a conservative estimate is thirty-two hundred men.

After Newtown the army continued its march practically unmolested. The Indians seemed to feel the hopelessness of staying its progress. It appeared at times as if a well directed attack would seriously cripple the army, passing as it did with difficulty through narrow defiles in a long and slender line of march and seriously encumbered with the beasts of burden and provisions. On September 1st, the army was in a swamp and Lieutenant Barton wrote in his diary,

Had the savages availed themselves of this opportunity, it must have proved very fatal to us, for they might with ease have destroyed a great part of our provisions with a party very inconsiderable.

Another officer wrote at about the same time:

I am sure that a few men of spirit might exceedingly retard our movements.

But the Indians had been badly beaten, and they believed the invading army which advanced with the greatest caution and whose numbers they exaggerated, was invincible. The fresh bands of warriors which occasionally joined them were eager to engage the army, but the fighting spirit of those who had been at Newtown was for the time utterly broken, and their tales of defeat effectually cooled the ardour of the new men. Nor did complete harmony of purpose exist in the Indian camp. There was a powerful faction which hoped to secure peace by taking a neutral stand; and it is said that some of the Indians, notably Red Jacket, then a young warrior, afterwards to become famous as an orator, attempted to enter into negotiations to that end.

Shortly after destroying and leaving Newtown, the army reached Catherines-town, the home of the celebrated Catherine Montour, on the site of the present village of Montour Falls and but two miles from Watkins, and the head of Seneca Lake. Here they found an aged squaw, the sole inhabitant of the deserted village, who told them that the defeat at Newtown had completely demoralized the Indian warriors. She was well treated by the officers. After the destruction of the village, a hut was erected, and provisions were left for her use. So bitter was the feeling of many of the rank and file against the Indians that it was with some difficulty that this old woman was protected from violence.

The course of the army was now northward along the east shore of Seneca Lake, 'The most beautiful I have ever seen,' said one of the officers. The country was comparatively level, and rapid progress was made. The trail led to the important Indian town of Kanadesaga, at the foot of the lake, very near where Geneva now stands. It was believed that the Indians had prepared to defend their town and a plan of attack was agreed upon. But when the men entered the village, they found there as its sole defender a little white boy, four or five years of age, nearly starved and entirely naked. He was tenderly cared for and adopted by the officers. The army then destroyed Kanadesaga with its fields of corn and its orchards of apple, peach and mulberry trees. General Sullivan now called a council to discuss the advisability of proceeding farther. The scarcity of provisions, the fact that the army since it began its march into the wilderness was completely cut off from its base of supplies, and the uncertainty of obtaining sufficient sustenance from the country through which it was passing, rendered a further advance dangerous.

The main object of the expedition, the intimidation of the Indians and the destruction of their principal settlements, seemed already to have been accomplished. Sullivan had been informed, however, that the principal village of the Senecas, the most numerous and formidable of the Iroquois, was on the Genesee River and that at that place were the largest and choicest fields and orchards and the greatest stores of provisions. These provisions, it was believed, were collected to sustain the British, as well as the Indian forces, and as the object of the campaign was to out off every possibility of attack from this quarter, a further advance was considered. The spirit of the army was excellent, the men cheerfully living on one-half rations, although these were abundantly supplemented by the products of the country through which they were marching. What was not used by the army was completely destroyed. It was decided to march to the Genesee.

The army following the trail closely, for there were no guides who could otherwise find their way through this country, moved to the westward and soon reached Kanandaigua, where the present village now is. From there the trail led to the southwest, passing to the north of Honeoye and Hemlock Lakes, and on the 12th of September the army arrived at the head of Cenesus Lake. Here was the Indian village of Kanaghsaws, the home of the famous chief. Big Tree. Sullivan now believed that he was near the great Seneca village of which he was in search and which was to mark the limit of the expedition, and he determined to explore the trail to the river before proceeding with the army.

While Sullivan's soldiers were burning the houses and cutting down the corn at the Indian village of Kanaghsaws, numbers of bark canoes, freighted with Indian warriors glided down the river, flowing now rapidly, now placidly through the valley which the Indians, with the appropriateness which characterizes their nomenclature, called the Genesee, the beautiful valley. Guided by skilful hand and practiced eye or driven onward by long and powerful sweeps of the paddle they moved rapidly down the river to the great Seneca village at the Western end of the Long House of the Iroquois.

The village was built on the west bank of the river, where Cuylerville now is, in the midst of acres of cultivated fields, and thousands of fruit-bearing trees. With the beautiful valley stretching to the north and to the south, and the magnificent forest scenery on every hand and enclosing all, the whole scene must have been one of peace and beauty. Well might Sullivan's soldiers believe that they had reached an earthly paradise; and the men who first sought this charming and fruitful country on an errand of death and destruction and left it in ruins and desolation came in later days with their families and the arts of peace to build it up again.

The river had reflected many a council fire, but never during the centuries that it, had floated the bark canoes of the Iroquois had the chiefs met on its banks in more solemn and anxious deliberation. But a few miles away a numerous army, spreading destruction in its path, was moving relentlessly onward and penetrating the fastnesses of the wilderness which had hitherto been considered impregnable. The most famous chiefs of the Confederacy were gathered around the council fire and their deliberations were conducted with characteristic solemnity and decorum, despite the near and rapid approach of the enemy, and the wailing of the frightened women and children.

The bolder spirits prevailed, and on the night of the 12th of September, the several bands of warriors under their favourite chiefs made their way out of the village and across the river to play their part in the attack which had been determined upon, and make a last and desperate effort in defence of their homes. They were animated with the courage of desperation and hardly with the hope of success. Mary

Jemison, the white captive of the Genesee, tells us that;

> . . . the women and children were sent into the woods to the west of the town in order that we might make a good retreat if it should be necessary.

It must have been with something like a feeling of despair that the warriors, scantily supported by the Tories, went out from their village to attack an enemy many times their number, better armed than themselves, active and vigilant, and flushed with success.

It was decided that the army should be led into an ambuscade, the favourite method of Indian warfare, and in its success lay their only hope of victory. If it failed, the only thing to be done was to make good their retreat, and for that all preparations had been made. The army had reached the head of Conesus Lake and was engaged in building a bridge over the inlet for the passage of the artillery, when the British and Indian forces took up their position on the hill to the west of the inlet. The trail along which the army must pass continued obliquely up the hill, and followed for nearly a mile the heads of numerous ravines which cut up the hillside.

The place chosen for the ambuscade was at the north of the trail which held a generally westerly direction, and at the heads of the ravines about three-quarters of a mile from a point where the army, unconscious of the presence of the enemy, was at work upon the bridge. The place was admirably chosen, and the plan appears to have been to permit part of the army to pass the place of ambuscade before beginning the attack. There, on the morning of September 13th with the Tories mingled with them, the Indians lay In their place of concealment, anxiously and impatiently watching the army make its leisurely preparations to cross the inlet and proceed along the trail.

But when the army marched past the heads of the ravines there were no Indians there to receive them. On the previous evening Lieutenant Boyd had been sent out by Sullivan with instructions to take with him four riflemen and an Indian guide and ascertain the location of the Genesee Castle, which was supposed to be on the east bank of the river. Boyd disregarded the first part of his instructions, and took with him twenty-eight men, including his guides. They passed quietly up the trail towards the river on the night of the 12th, probably before the Indians had taken up their position at the point of ambuscade, and went on unmolested and undiscovered. They continued on the direct trail, and in the evening arrived at the Indian village of Gathtsegwarohare, a short distance east of the river, instead of at the Genesee Castle, which they expected to find.

The old Indian village of Chenussio which was shown on the maps in Sullivan's possession and which was located on the east bank of the Genesee at the junction of the Canaseraga Creek with the river was no longer in existence. Boyd found Gathtsegwarohare abandoned, and after sending back two men to report that fact to Sullivan, determined to await there the advance of the army. Some straggling Indians were fired upon by the party, one of whom was killed, and then thinking that it would be safer to rejoin the army, Boyd started back along the trail. More Indians were seen, and these at the sight of Boyd's party, instead of disappearing into the woods, lured Boyd in pursuit directly Into the lines of the ambuscade. Boyd and his men fought bravely against fearful odds, but nearly all of them were killed or captured.

The Indians who had been for hours lying in their cover, awaiting the advance of the main army, heard with dismay the heavy firing in their rear. Having no knowledge of the size of Boyd's force they believed they were surrounded, and those who did not go to the assistance of the party that had attacked Boyd made their way hastily to the river. When the truth was learned It was too late to take up their old position. An incautious Indian had fired upon the surveyor's party which had pushed ahead of the main army, and an immediate advance was ordered, Sullivan soon learning from one of Boyd's men who escaped, of the disaster to his scouting party.

The ambuscade had completely failed. Another council was immediately held in the face of the advancing army and the bolder warriors were in favor of making still another and desperate effort to check the foe. But a majority of the Indians had already deserted, and all were impressed with the hopelessness of the struggle. When Sullivan was about to enter the village of Gathtsegwarohare, a few of them were still drawn up in battle array, but they rapidly melted away before the advancing columns of the army. All resistance was now at an end and Sullivan, unmolested, pushed his way to the Genesee Castle. Now the path of the army lay along the Genesee flats on the east side of the river, 'containing' says Major Fogg, 'about 20,000 acres with not a stump nor a tree upon the whole, but grass six to ten feet high.'

Colonel Henry Dearborn wrote,

Our army appeared there to a very great advantage moving in the exact order of march laid down in the plan but very often we who were on horseback could see nothing but the men's guns above the grass.

The river was soon reached and forded and from an eminence on the west side the army had a view of the great town of the Senecas of which General Sullivan in his official report says,

> The castle consisted of 128 houses, mostly large and elegant. The place was beautifully situated, almost encircled with a cleared flat which extended for a number of miles, where the most extensive fields of corn were waving, and every kind of vegetable that can be conceived.

The army marched into the town on the 14th of September and immediately began its work of destruction.

Hardly had they entered the village, when they discovered the headless bodies of Boyd and a private named Parker, who was captured with him by the Indians. Parker had been apparently killed at once, but Boyd's body was terribly mutilated and he had been subjected to the most exquisite tortures. They were buried with military honours. Much has been written of Boyd's appeal for protection to the famous Mohawk chief, Brant, on the score of free masonry, and of his being put to the torture only after that chief's departure from the village, and on Boyd's patriotic refusal to give information of the numbers and plans of the Americans. There seems to be no authentic corroboration of this tale.

On the other hand, Butler the Tory leader wrote to headquarters, that Boyd informed him that Sullivan had a force of 5,000 men and that its destination was the Genesee Castle. He adds that the officer appeared to be intelligent and well informed. Terrible as Boyd's fate was his torture was but a natural outbreak of the hatred of the Indian warriors against the enemy that was laying waste their country. The misfortune to the scouting party was probably the means of saving the army; or at least, of preventing a much greater loss of life. Had Boyd in the first instance taken with him but the four men he was directed to take, they probably would have been killed or captured without drawing the main body of the Indians from their ambuscade. Had he returned with his whole force to the main army at the time he sent two of his men to report to Sullivan, he would have returned unmolested and with his report that the path was clear and the Indian village abandoned, the army probably would have marched confidently along the trail and fallen into the trap laid for it.

Had he instead of going to the village of Gathtsegwarohare followed the other trail to the old Chenussio, he probably would have been attacked so far from the main force that the Indians in ambuscade would not have been demoralized. What actually would have occurred in these contingencies we can only conjecture; but the desperate fight to the death made by Boyd and his men was the means of disorganizing the Indian and Tory forces and consequently spoiling their plan for attacking the army.

There was no more fighting. The Genesee Castle was burned; its thousands of fruit trees were destroyed; and the corn and vegetables cut down and thrown into the river. So thoroughly was the work of destruction done, that Mary Jemison tells us that on the Indians returning to take possession of the village:

> What were our feelings when we found that there was not a mouthful of sustenance left, not even enough to keep a child one day from perishing from hunger.

She also said that

> Our corn was good that year, a part of which we had gathered and secured for winter.

The fruitfulness of the country was a constant marvel to the men of Sullivan's army, many of whom, in times of peace, wrung their livelihood from the more sterile soil of the Eastern Colonies. The principal product of the Indians was corn, which was ripening when destroyed by the army. Lieutenant Beatty wrote in his diary on August 30th, 'Our brigade destroyed about 150 acres of the best corn that I ever saw (some of the stalks grew sixteen feet high,)' and another officer wrote on the same day that 'The land exceeds any that I have ever seen. Some corn stalks measured eighteen feet, and a cob one foot and a half long.' The vegetables, found in great quantities, were beans, cucumbers, watermelons, pumpkins, onions, squash, turnips, cabbages, carrots and parsnips. Along the east bank of Seneca Lake were great fields of pea vines.

The orchards, some of which were very large, containing as many as 1,500 trees, were principally apple and peach. Were it not for this quantity of corn, vegetables and fruits found on every hand, the army must have turned back long before reaching the Genesee Valley. The day after the battle of Newtown, an order was issued that the men draw only half rations; and on arriving at Kanadesaga, now Geneva, Major Burroughs wrote 'The country abounds with corn and beans, which we solely live on;' and later, 'Corn and beans plenty, which is now of great consequence to us.'

General Sullivan reported that 'The quantity of corn destroyed, at a moderate computation, must amount to 160,000 bushels, with a vast quantity of vegetables of every kind.'

After the destruction of the Genesee Castle was completed the army began its homeward march, returning the same way it came. No more hostile Indians were seen, A party was detached from the main army to destroy the corn, which had not been cut down on the west side of Seneca lake, and another body of 600 men, under Colonel Butler, circled Cayuga Lake and destroyed the villages of the Cayugas and hundreds of acres of corn and orchards. When the campaign was over. General Sullivan reported to congress in the following words: 'It is with pleasure I inform the congress that this army has not suffered the loss of forty men in action or otherwise since my taking the command; though, perhaps, few troops have experienced a more fatiguing campaign.

Besides the difficulties which naturally attended marching through an enemy's country, abounding in woods, creeks, rivers, mountains, morasses and defiles, we found no small inconvenience from the want of proper guides, and the maps of the country are so exceedingly erroneous that they serve not to enlighten, but to perplex. We had not a person who was sufficiently acquainted with the country to conduct a party out of the Indian path by day or scarcely in it by night; though they were the best I possibly could procure. Their ignorance doubtless arose from the Indians having ever taken the best measures in their power to prevent their country's being explored.

We had much labour in clearing out the roads for the artillery, notwithstanding which the army moved from twelve to sixteen miles every day, when not detained by rains or employed in destroying settlements. The number of towns destroyed by this army amounted to forty besides scattering houses. Every creek and river has been traced, and the whole country explored in search of Indian settlements, and I am well persuaded that, except one town situated near Allegana, about fifty miles from Chinesse, there is not a single town left in the country of the Five Nations."

Sullivan had apparently done all that he was ordered to do with one exception. He had made no captives, and had killed very few Indians. But this was hardly his fault. Except at Newtown he had seen very few Indians to kill or capture. They had constantly watched the army on its course, from their points of vantage back from the beaten trail's; but there the army could not follow them. The destruction of the settlements and crops had been very complete, although there were three villages instead of one, as stated by Sullivan, that were not entered and destroyed by the army. The most important of these was a town on the Genesee River, where Avon now is, which was called by the Indians, on account of the sulphur springs in the vicinity, Canewaugus, meaning literally, 'stinking water.' The Indians had also managed to conceal, before the arrival of the army, the portion of their crops which had already been gathered.

Successful though the campaign was in the manner of its execution, its results were not what it was hoped or expected that they would be. The greater part of the Indians journeyed to the fort at Niagara, after abandoning the Genesee Castle. From there on September 20th, Colonel Bolton wrote to General Haldimand, the British commander at Montreal:

> Butler assures me that if 500 men had joined the Rangers in time, instead of 300, at least 1,000 warriors would have turned out and with this force he is convinced Mr. Sullivan would have had some reason to repent his expedition. But the Indians, not being supported, as they expected, they thought of nothing more than carrying off their families.

And Butler himself wrote at about the same time:

> The reinforcements your Excellency is sending out are too late to save the country of the Five Nations. This has been very rapidly effected by the rebels, whose superior strength and numbers made all efforts to stop their progress of small avail.
> Notwithstanding their losses, the Indians seem unshaken in their attachment to His Majesty's cause.
> They are bringing their families with them, and after leaving them at Niagara, will return for revenge.

The measures taken by congress to punish the Iroquois were so severe that it would seem that there could be little hope of their remaining neutral during the remainder of the war. That some such idea was held by Washington is evidenced by a letter that he wrote on January 30, 1780, to General Schuyler. He said,

> The hour of victory, we are informed by Lord North, is the time for negotiation. That hour, so far as they (the Iroquois) are concerned, is come, and it would be wrong, in my judgement, to force them irrevocably in the arms of the enemy. To compel

a people to remain in a state of desperation, and to keep them at enmity with us when no good is to be expected from it and much evil may follow, is playing the whole game against us.

But Sullivan's work had been too well done. In the spring of 1780, Colonel Bolton wrote to Haldimand,

Had Sullivan acted with more prudence and less severity, I am satisfied that we should not have had one-third of the Six Nations in our interest at this time.

The winter of 1779 and '80, was one of great severity, and it is said that in Western New York and Upper Canada the snow fell to a depth of nearly eight feet. The sufferings of the Indians from disease and want of adequate provisions were intense. Hardly had the spring opened, however, than the Iroquois began their depredations on the frontier settlements with an eagerness and ferocity born of anger and revenge. The inhabitants of the frontier who had abandoned their homes in fear the year before were led to believe that the blow given by Sullivan crushed out forever the spirit of the Indian tribes; and lulled into security they again took up their lives on the outskirts of the settlements.

Unfortunately, they little understood the indomitable spirit and wonderful vitality of the Iroquois, reduced though they were in numbers and power. The revenge taken by the Indians for the desolation left by Sullivan's army, though not so complete, may be compared with the terrible retaliation of the Iroquois nations on the French settlements at Montreal after the destructive campaign of the French under De Nonville into the Iroquois country, in 1687. Mary Jemison tells the story of one of the first of these expeditions as follows:

The next summer after Sullivan's campaign, our Indians, highly incensed at the whites for the treatment they had received, and the sufferings which they had consequently endured, determined to obtain some redress by destroying their frontier settlements. Cornplanter, otherwise called John O'Ball led the Indians. An officer by the name of Johnson commanded the British in the expedition. The force was large, and so strongly bent on retaliation that apparently nothing could avert its march or prevent its depredations.

After leaving Genesee they marched directly to some of the headwaters of the Susquehanna River and Schoharie Creek, went down that creek to the Mohawk River; thence up that river to Port Stanwix and from thence came home. In their route they burned a number of places, destroyed all the cattle and other property that came in their way, killed a number of white people and brought home a few prisoners.

These expeditions, or raids against the frontier settlements continued until the close of the war. After Sullivan's campaign the Iroquois were the implacable enemies of the colonists. In July, 1780, Colonel Guy Johnson wrote to General Haldimand at Montreal,

Sullivan's announcement to congress that the Six Nations are humbled and the frontier secure proved to be an error. The Indians are in high spirits from the hope of reducing the rebels.

The English officers made many unsuccessful attempts to restrain their ferocity. In August, 1782, Captain Powell wrote to Montreal from Niagara

The shocking cruelties of the Indians have been ordered to be stopped. The rebel prisoners shall be sent down as soon as collected.

It can well be understood that these orders, had but little effect on the revengeful spirit of the Iroquois.

Sullivan has been severely criticized for not pushing on to Niagara and capturing the fort there, which was the principal stronghold of the British in this section, and the point at which were organized the destructive Indian expeditions of the later years of the war. He was not directed to do so in his instructions and there were good military reasons for abandoning the project

If he seriously considered it. The limited stock of provisions carried by the army would not warrant it; the season was too far advanced; and if he had succeeded in reaching Niagara and taking the fort. It would have been impossible for the army to exist there entirely cut off from any base of supplies. A Colonial army, in the wilds of Western New York, during the severe winter of 1779-80 would have suffered disaster more crushing than that of Napoleon's in its invasion of Russia.

But the ultimate results of this expedition into the country of the Iroquois were vastly different in character, and more far reaching than were conceived of by the men who planned it. It opened the eyes of the people of the Colonies to the beauty and capabilities of this great section of our state. No sooner had war ended, than colonization began; and the nations of the Iroquois which had held this country for centuries against the attack of warlike foes, were rapidly and completely subdued and driven from their hunting grounds by the army of civilization.